Your New Life
with Christ

Gal 2 : 20

Your New Life with Christ

LUIS PALAU

AND LUIS PALAU EVANGELISTIC ASSOCIATION

CROSSWAY BOOKS • WHEATON, ILLINOIS
A DIVISION OF GOOD NEWS PUBLISHERS

Your New Life with Christ

Copyright © 1996 by Luis Palau and Luis Palau Evangelistic Association

Published by Crossway Books
    a division of Good News Publishers
    1300 Crescent Street
    Wheaton, Illinois 60187

Original edition copyright © 1989 by Luis Palau Evangelistic Association

All teaching articles in this book are written by Luis Palau and have been excerpted and adapted from his previously published works. Used by permission.

Sessions 1-6 in Part II are adapted from *Living as a Christian*, copyright © 1982, 1985, 1991 British & Foreign Bible Society and Scripture Union and used with permission.

The Gospel of Luke in Part IV and biblical quotations throughout this book, unless otherwise indicated, are taken from the HOLY BIBLE: NEW INTERNATIONAL VERSION. Copyright © 1973, 1978, 1984 by International Bible Society. Used by permission of Zondervan Publishing House. All rights reserved.

The "NIV" and "New International Version" trademarks are registered in the United States Patent and Trademark Office by International Bible Society. Use of either trademark requires the permission of International Bible Society.

Cover design: Cindy Kiple

First printing, 1996

Printed in the United States of America

Library of Congress Cataloging-in-Publication Data
Palau, Luis, 1934-
    Your new life with Christ / Luis Palau Evangelistic Association.
      p.   cm.
    ISBN 0-89107-871-1
    1. Church membership.   2. Christian life.   I. Luis Palau
Evangelistic Association.   II. Title.
BV4520.P25 1996
248.4—dc20   95-45413

04		03		02		01		00		99						
15	14	13	12	11	10	9	8	7	6	5	4	3	2				

A N   I N V I T A T I O N

If you have recently committed your life to the Lord Jesus Christ, if you have come to know Him as your personal Savior and have received forgiveness of your sins from Him, this book is for you. Congratulations! You have taken the most important step in your life. You've begun an exciting journey that only gets better. Think of *Your New Life with Christ* as a spiritual map to help direct you in your new walk with Christ. If we may be of further assistance, please write to us. Our address is P.O. Box 1173, Portland, Oregon 97207.

Luis Palau

CONTENTS

INTRODUCTION:
A Word of Encouragement from Luis Palau / 9

PART I: COMING TO CHRIST

PART II: GROWING IN CHRIST

A Word of Encouragement from Luis Palau

How wonderful it is to experience a vital, living, personal relationship with the Lord Jesus Christ! Even though you may just now have become a Christian—or you may be returning to a fresh, new relationship with Jesus Christ after a period of doubt or difficult circumstances—you can enjoy a wonderful experience with the Lord today and tomorrow and the next day and . . .

The Lord Jesus says, "I have come that they may have life, and have it to the full" (John 10:10). He has promised us an abundant and enjoyable life, and He has made every provision for us to live that life.

Here are some practical ways to enjoy a deep and fulfilling relationship with Jesus Christ.

(1) *Begin reading God's Word,* the Bible, each day. Start with the Gospel of Luke, which is printed in Part IV of this book.

(2) *Talk to God in prayer daily.* Thank Him for what He has done—and wants to do—in your life.

(3) *Begin attending a local church* where Jesus Christ is preached and God's love for others is demonstrated.

(4) *Tell someone else about Jesus Christ,* and pray that he or she will receive Christ as personal Savior and Lord.

You may also find it helpful to write out your story. This is good practice and will make it easier to tell others about your new life in Christ.

I hope you enjoy reading and using this book, which I believe will help you get to know Jesus Christ better and to walk more closely with Him. You will notice that some sections have been prepared by me and my staff and that some sections have been written by me personally. So when you read "I" and "me," that's from me to you.

My prayer for you is that you will always want to live your life to the honor and glory of God and His Son, the Lord Jesus Christ!

Coming to Christ

▼

My Commitment

MY COMMITMENT 1
▼

The following statement best describes the decision I am making (check one):

❑ I recently prayed to receive Jesus Christ as my Savior. I now desire to confess that decision publicly. (Please see pages 14-16)

❑ I have received Jesus Christ as my Savior but don't have assurance that my sins are forgiven and that I have eternal life. I would like biblical assurance of salvation. (Please see pages 14-15 and 18.)

❑ I have received Jesus Christ as my Savior, but I have failed Him. I desire to rededicate my life to Him. (Please turn to pages 14-15 and 17.)

❑ I have heard the Gospel message and I am very interested in receiving Jesus Christ, but I have not yet made a decision. (Please turn to page 14.)

❑ I have a special need I would like to discuss with someone.

MY COMMITMENT 2

Let's review the basic facts of the Gospel. Perhaps you already have trusted Jesus Christ as your own Savior. But it is always helpful to review the step we took and what happened in our soul when we did.

(1) God's Plan—Peace and Life

God loves you and wants you to fully experience the peace and life that only He can give. The Bible says, "For God so loved the world that he gave his one and only Son [Jesus Christ], that whoever believes in him shall not perish but have eternal life" (John 3:16).

(2) Humanity's Problem—Separation

Being at peace with God is not automatic, because human beings by nature are separated from God. The Bible says, "All have sinned and fall short of the glory of God" (Romans 3:23). Romans 6:23 adds: "The wages of sin is death, but the gift of God is eternal life in Christ Jesus our Lord." Humanity has tried to bridge this separation in many ways . . . without success.

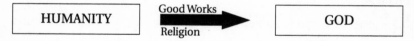

(3) God's Remedy—the Cross

God's love bridges the gap of separation between God and humanity. When Jesus Christ died on the cross and rose from the grave, He paid the penalty for our sins. In the Bible, Jesus Christ says, "I am the way and the truth and the life. No one comes to the Father except through me" (John 14:6).

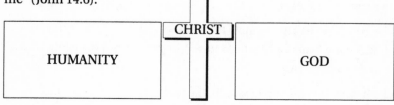

(4) Our Response—Receive Jesus Christ

God invites us to respond to His love by crossing the bridge through trusting Jesus Christ. This means accepting Christ's death on the cross as payment for our personal sins and receiving Him as our Savior and Lord. The Bible says, "To all who received him [Jesus Christ], to those who believed in his name, he gave the right to become children of God" (John 1:12).

The Invitation Was To:

Repent (turn from your sins), by faith receive Jesus Christ into your heart and life, and follow Him in obedience as the Lord of your life.

What to Pray:

O God, I know I am a sinner. Right now I repent and turn from my sins. I believe Jesus Christ died for my sins, rose from the grave, and is alive forever. I open the door of my heart and life, receiving Jesus Christ as my Savior. I want to follow Him as Lord of my life. Thank You for saving me. Amen.

MY COMMITMENT 3

Receiving Jesus Christ as Savior and Lord
You have prayed to receive Jesus Christ. You have asked Jesus Christ
to come into your life. What does the Bible say happened?

In the Bible Jesus Christ says, "Here I am! I stand at the door and
knock. If anyone hears my voice and opens the door, I will come in
and eat with him, and he with me" (Revelation 3:20).

What did Jesus Christ say He would do if you asked Him in?
"I will_____."
So where is He right now? _____

_____

What happened when you received Christ?

The Bible says, ". . . to all who received him [Jesus Christ], he
[God] gave the right to become children of God. All they needed to do
was to trust him to save them. All those who believe this are reborn!"
(John 1:12-13, *The Living Bible*).

What did you become when you received Jesus Christ? _____

_____

The Bible also says, "If you confess with your mouth, 'Jesus is
Lord,' and believe in your heart that God raised him from the dead,
you will be saved" (Romans 10:9).

What does this verse promise to those who confess and believe
in Jesus Christ?
"You will _____."

How do you know . . .	*I know because . . .*
that Christ came in?	God said it . . . in His Word.
you are a child of God?	I believe it . . . in my heart.
you are saved?	That settles it . . . in my mind.

Additional Scripture Verses
Acts 16:31, John 3:16, Ephesians 2:8-9, Romans 10:13, Romans 6:23.

MY COMMITMENT 4

Rededication or Restoration
You say you have received Jesus Christ before, but are coming to rededicate your life to Him. You may have failed Him and you are seeking His forgiveness.

Here's How to Be Forgiven
The Bible says, "If we confess our sins, he [God] is faithful and just and will forgive us our sins and purify us from all unrighteousness" (1 John 1:9).

Note: The word "confess" means to agree with God ... I lied ... I cheated ... I was unkind ... I lost my temper.

What must we do to be forgiven? _____

What does God say He will do if we confess? _____

Right now take time to be specific with God ... confess your sins.

Steps to Follow Confession
The Bible says, "He who conceals his sins does not prosper, but whoever confesses and renounces them finds mercy" (Proverbs 28:13).

What happens if we try to conceal or hide our sins?

We _____.

Following confession we must _____ our sins.

Note: The Apostle Paul said, "I strive always to keep my conscience clear before God and man" (Acts 24:16).

If you have wronged someone, you need to make it right not only with God, but also with the one you have wronged. Do it soon.

How do you know ...	*I know because ...*
you are forgiven?	God said it ... in His Word.
you are cleansed?	I believe it ... in my heart.
you are restored?	That settles it ... in my mind.

Additional Scripture Verses
Psalm 32:5, 1 John 2:1-2, Psalm 66:18.

MY COMMITMENT 5

Assurance of Salvation

You say you have received Jesus Christ as your Savior but lack assurance of eternal life. Look at these promises . . .

The Bible says, "For God so loved the world that he gave his one and only Son [Jesus Christ], that whoever believes in him shall not perish but have eternal life" (John 3:16).

What does God promise you? _____

What did God give to make eternal life possible? _____

What must you do to possess eternal life? _____

In the Bible, Jesus Christ says, "My sheep listen to my voice; I know them, and they follow me. I give them eternal life, and they shall never perish; no one can snatch them out of my hand" (John 10:27-28).

What are you promised?

"I give them _____."

"And they shall never _____."

"No one can _____ them out of my _____."

How do you know . . .	*I know because . . .*
you have eternal life?	God said it . . . in His Word.
you will never perish?	I believe it . . . in my heart.
you are safe in God's hand?	That settles it . . . in my mind.

Additional Scripture Verses

Ephesians 1:7, John 5:24, Romans 8:38-39.

▼

Bible Study Lesson One: Learning More About Jesus Christ

The new life you now possess is based on your relationship with Jesus Christ. The purpose of this lesson is to encourage that relationship by helping you deepen your understanding of who He is and by helping you discover the fullness of His free gift of eternal life.

As you work through this lesson, you will discover that the Bible has the answers to some of life's most important questions. It also reveals God's great love for you and His plan for your life. The keys to unlocking the treasures of the Bible are reading it daily, studying it carefully, and memorizing verses that can help you from day to day. This lesson will give you the opportunity to practice each of these basic disciplines of the Christian life.

Jesus said, "I have come that they may have life, and have it to the full" (John 10:10). We pray that you will experience the abundance of your new life in Christ today and will continue to grow in it always.

INSTRUCTIONS

Answer the following questions using the Gospel of Luke printed in

Part IV of this book. The references will help you locate the verses. For example, you'll find Luke 4:32 in:

> Luke—the book of the Bible
> 4—the specific chapter in that book
> 32—the specific verse in that chapter.

After you read the verses, try to answer each question in your own words.

THE NATURE AND MISSION OF JESUS CHRIST

(1) Why was Jesus sent into the world? See Luke 5:17-26.

_____

_____

_____

  In the book of Luke, Jesus often is referred to as the "Son of Man."

(2) Some say Jesus was only a man, but others say He was also God. What does the Bible say? See Luke 2:11.

_____

_____

  See Luke 22:70.

_____

_____

ETERNAL LIFE IN JESUS CHRIST

(1) What is God's attitude toward those who are lost without Jesus Christ? See Luke 15:4-7.

_____

_____

(2) How does a person receive eternal life? See Luke 7:48.

_____

_____

See Luke 7:50.

_____

_____

To believe in Jesus Christ means more than agreeing with what the Bible says about Him. To believe in Jesus is to choose to trust Him alone for eternal life. You can't earn eternal life by performing good deeds or religious works. It is important to understand that Jesus alone can forgive your sins and give you eternal life.

YOUR RELATIONSHIP WITH JESUS CHRIST

Briefly describe how you received Jesus Christ as your Savior and how you know for certain that you have eternal life.

_____

_____

_____

_____

_____

_____

_____

_____

_____

_____

_____

MEMORIZE THIS PROMISE

"For the Son of Man came to seek and to save what was lost."
Luke 19:10

▼

Bible Study Lesson Two: Living the Christian Life

As you begin or continue your new life in Christ, you can do three things to encourage your spiritual growth.

(1) Let God speak to you through His Word, the Bible. As you read the Bible, you will discover that it talks about everyday issues in a practical manner. Through His Word, God can help you with each and every area of your life.

(2) Speak to God by praying every day. You can talk to God about anything. He is always available and willing to listen to you.

(3) Speak to others about God. You began your new life in Christ because someone took the time to tell you about Jesus. Now you have the opportunity to tell others what Jesus has done in your life.

Today, begin to grow spiritually by reading your Bible, praying, and telling others what Jesus has done for you. This lesson will help you understand why these elements are essential for spiritual growth.

INSTRUCTIONS

Read the following verses in the Gospel of Luke in Part IV of this book. Then answer the questions in your own words.

THE BIBLE—GOD SPEAKING TO US

Jesus says this about God's Word: "It is written: 'Man does not live on bread alone, but on every word that comes from the mouth of God'" (Matthew 4:4).

(1) What will God's Word do for a person? See Luke 6:46-49.

_____

_____

_____

(2) What is the result of doing what the Bible says? See Luke 11:28.

_____

_____

_____

(4) Will we always have God's Word to instruct and encourage us in the Christian life? Why? See Luke 21:33.

_____

_____

PRAYER—SPEAKING TO GOD

(1) In Luke 11:1-4, the disciples asked Jesus to teach them to pray. List some of His suggestions for subjects of prayer. See Luke 11:2.

_____

_____

See Luke 11:3.

_____

_____

See Luke 11:4.

_____

_____

(2) What does Jesus go on to say about prayer? See Luke 11:9-10.

_____

_____

See Luke 11:11-13.

_____

_____

(3) List one area of your Christian life that can be helped with prayer. See Luke 22:40, 46.

_____

_____

_____

(4) What important truth about prayer do we discover from Jesus' prayer the night before His crucifixion? See Luke 22:42.

_____

_____

_____

WITNESSING—SPEAKING TO OTHERS ABOUT GOD

(1) Why did Jesus come to earth? See Luke 5:31-32.

_____

_____

_____

(2) What does Jesus tell us to do in response to what He has done for us? See Luke 8:39.

_____

_____

_____

(3) What is the point of Jesus' parable about the Good Samaritan? See Luke 10:30-37.

_____

_____

_____

(4) Some of the last words Jesus spoke before He ascended into

heaven are recorded in Luke 24:46-48. What did Jesus say we should be?

Luke 24:46-48 _____

MEMORIZE THIS PROMISE

"Blessed rather are those who hear the word of God and obey it."

Luke 11:28

Growing in Christ

▼

Welcome to God's Family!

I am so glad you have committed your life to Jesus Christ. An exciting thing happened when you took that step of faith. You became part of God's family. As in any loving family, we all need one another. Our Christian family helps us learn how to live God's way.

Nurture groups—whether home Bible studies, small groups, adult Sunday school classes, or new believer discipleship groups formed after an evangelistic crusade—effectively help new Christians become anchored in their faith. It is important for your spiritual growth and your walk with Christ that you seek out and join such a group.

If you do not know of an existing nurture group, talk with a pastor or another experienced Christian you know who would be able to help begin such a group. A nurture group can be as small as two or three believers in Christ, or as large as a dozen. (Generally speaking, twelve should be the maximum group size to maintain an atmosphere of relaxed fellowship, acceptance, and open sharing.)

In a nurture group you will have an opportunity to meet with other newer Christians like yourself, as well as more mature believers who have been following Christ for a number of years. As you get to know these other Christians and as you explore the relevance of God's Word with them, you will grow in your relationship with Christ.

At times you may feel like giving up. But the Christian family in your group will encourage you, listen to you, answer your questions, and show their Christian love for you. In a nurture group you can expect to receive help and also to give it.

Your Christian family will bring you closer to God. You and the others will pray together and worship God together. You will learn to experience deep joy as you meet with one another.

Being part of a nurture group is exciting! You will gain a lot from your group, and you will give a lot. In fact, the more you give, the more you will get. The following six sessions are designed for group use and are to be undertaken carefully and prayerfully. So take time to prepare for each meeting and to think and pray about what you have learned. Expect God to speak to you through His Holy Spirit—and He will!

Luis Palau

▼

Session One: Beginnings

THE GOAL

Sharing with others can be helpful and encouraging. In a nurture group, you will discover how other members received Christ and how God has helped them in their daily lives. You also will learn about God and how to worship and praise Him.

AT THE GROUP

Share

You will have the opportunity to tell others how you decided to follow Christ and what you have discovered about Him. It may help if you write out answers to questions similar to these:

Can you think of one word to describe how you felt when you made your commitment to Christ?

What helped you take this step?

How is it working out? How has Christ made a difference in your life?

Pray

You will be able to pray silently or aloud for other group members. Try to remember some of their specific prayer requests and pray about them as they come to mind. If you have sensed God saying anything new to you, silently thank Him for it, and ask Him to help you act on it.

DURING THE WEEK

Read Luke 23:39-49, and come prepared to share your answers to next week's questions. Set aside time each day to pray and read the Bible, beginning with the Gospel of Luke in Part IV of this book. As you read, mark one meaningful verse you can share with the group next week. Now that Christ lives in you, you never will make decisions or face problems alone again. When a decision or problem arises, ask God to help you. If you have any questions throughout the coming week, don't hesitate to contact your nurture group leader.

The Most Important Decision

Beginning your new life in Jesus Christ was a life-changing step! For the rest of your life you will be able to tell the story of how you committed your life to Christ. I'd like to share my story with you.

At age twelve I committed my life to Jesus Christ at a summer camp in the mountains of Argentina. Every night during camp Mr. Chandler, the counselor in my tent, would wake up one of us boys and—with a Bible in one hand and a flashlight in the other—take that boy outside. There, under the stars, he would lead the boy to faith in Christ.

Even though I felt guilty for my sins and knew I needed to commit my life to Christ, I didn't want to face the issue of eternity. But eventually every other boy in my tent had talked to Mr. Chandler. When he came into the tent that last night of camp, I knew why.

I pretended I was asleep, thinking he would go away. It didn't work. "Come on, Palau," he said, "get up." We went outside and sat down on a fallen tree.

"Luis," Mr. Chandler asked, "are you a Christian or not?"

I said, "I don't think so."

"It's not a matter of whether or not you think so. Are you or aren't you?"

"No, I'm not."

"If you died tonight, would you go to heaven or hell?"

I sat quietly for a moment before answering, "I'm going to hell."

"Is that where you want to go?"

"No," I replied.

"Then why are you going there?"

I shrugged my shoulders. "I don't know."

Mr. Chandler then turned his Bible to Romans and read: "If you confess with your lips, Luis, that Jesus is Lord and believe in your heart, Luis, that God raised him from the dead, you, Luis, will be saved. For man believes with his heart and so is justified, and he confesses with his lips and so is saved" (Romans 10:9-10, RSV).

He looked up at me. "Luis, do you believe in your heart that God raised Jesus from the dead?"

"Yes, I do," I replied.

"Then what do you have to do next to be saved?"

I hesitated, so Mr. Chandler had me read Romans 10:9 once more—"If you confess with your lips that Jesus is Lord . . . you will be saved."

Mr. Chandler then put his arm around me and led me in prayer. I opened my heart to Christ as we sat on that log in the rain. I was only twelve years old, but I knew I was saved. I had eternal life because Christ said, "I give them eternal life, and they shall never perish; no one can snatch them out of my hand" (John 10:28).

I could hardly sleep, I was so excited about committing my life to Christ! After all, that is the most important decision anyone can ever make. And I am so glad that you, too, have made that all-important decision!

Session Two: Being Sure

THE GOAL

God is always true to His Word. This week we will discover how His promises are proving true in the lives of other group members. We also will learn to appreciate how Jesus cares for us, guiding and protecting us in our daily lives.

AT THE GROUP

Read

Luke 23:39-49 shows us we can be sure of Jesus and His love for us because of what He has done for us.

Discuss

(1) What did the army officer (the centurion) think about Jesus? How could he have been so sure?

(2) In verse 46 what word best describes Jesus' attitude to His Father?

Doubting	Confident
Bitter	Resigned

▼

If you were going through a difficult time, how might Jesus' example help you?

(3) What did Jesus promise the dying thief in verse 43? How would you have felt if you had been that thief?

(4) Jesus accepted, loved, and forgave a man who was condemned as a criminal. What does that say about His attitude toward you?

Pray

Talk to God silently or aloud for the person sitting on either side of you, remembering a need that was shared earlier.

DURING THE WEEK

Read Luke 8:4-15 and prepare to share your answers to next week's questions.

Pray each day for at least one other group member. Remember a specific prayer request that the person shared, and use it as the basis for your prayers for him or her.

Claiming God's Promises for Yourself

As you read and study, memorize and meditate on various passages in the Bible, what sections seem the most difficult to believe? If you are like many Christians, it's most difficult for you to believe the promises of God. Oh, they sound nice, and sometimes they even cheer us up. But we also sometimes wonder, "Does God keep His promises?"

The answer is, yes, He does. In the Old Testament we read, "Not one of all the Lord's good promises to the house of Israel failed; every one was fulfilled" (Joshua 21:45; compare 23:14-15). Solomon later declared, "Praise be to the Lord, who has given rest to his people Israel just as he promised. Not one word has failed of all the good promises he gave through his servant Moses" (1 Kings 8:56). None of God's promises have ever failed!

The only absolutes we can proclaim are those found in God's Word. Throughout the Bible God has given His people "very great and precious promises" (2 Peter 1:4). Some of His promises were for specific individuals (see, for example, Joshua 14:9), a group (Deuteronomy 15:18), or a particular nation (Haggai 1:13). We must be careful not to haphazardly claim promises intended for someone else, but should confidently claim those promises that are meant for us as Christians.

Many Old Testament promises are repeated in the New Testament and are ours to enjoy and put to work today. For example, God promised Joshua, "I will never leave you or forsake you" (Joshua 1:5). In Hebrews 13:5 God transfers that promise to us as Christians.

The nineteenth-century evangelist Charles Spurgeon said, "O man, I beseech you, do not treat God's promises as if they were curiosities for a museum; but believe them and use them." We appropriate God's promises by learning them through the study and memorization of God's Word, by seeing our need for them, and by giving God time and opportunity to fulfill them in our daily lives.

God has promised to meet our every need. But we must ask for His provision. Any of God's promises that we can claim in Jesus' name are guaranteed and will be performed for us by God for His glory (John 14:13-14; 2 Corinthians 1:20).

What is the need of your heart today? The Lord has promised to meet that need! Simply take Him at His Word!

▼

Session Three:
Growing

THE GOAL

You may be surprised to discover how much you have learned about Jesus and how your relationship with Him has grown since you became a Christian. As we share together, we will find new ways in which we can continue growing.

AT THE GROUP

Pray

Under each of these headings list one or two specific prayer requests:

Praise	Family
Thanks	Others
Confession	Yourself

Use these categories to form short prayers. Remember, God is more interested in us than in special words or formulas for prayer.

Read

Do a careful, prayerful reading of Luke 8:4-15.

Jesus often taught truths in the form of stories or parables. These verses teach us some important lessons about growing as Christians. To benefit, we must apply these lessons to our daily lives.

Discuss

(1) Verse 12: Once we have heard the truth about Jesus, what might make us forget it?

(2) Verse 13: We all feel tempted at some point to go back on our commitment. How can we help one another keep our faith and joy alive?

(3) Verse 14: List the thorns that might be in your life.

(4) Verse 15: What must we do if we are to grow properly?

(5) What changes will these lessons make to the values and priorities we adopt in life?

DURING THE WEEK

Continue reading a portion of Luke every day. If you find a verse that means a lot to you, be prepared to share the verse with the other group members.

Read Luke 5:1-11, and prepare to share your answers to next week's questions.

Pray every day that God will help you get to know Him better.

▼

Doing What
Our Father Says

More than ninety people searched all night for Dominic DeCarlo, an eight-year-old boy lost on a snowy mountain while skiing with his father. With each passing hour the search party and the boy's parents became increasingly concerned for his health and safety.

By dawn they had found no trace of him. Then two helicopter crews joined the search, and within fifteen minutes they spotted ski tracks that changed to small footprints. The footprints led to a tree, where they found Dominic. Amazingly, he was in such good condition that he wasn't even hospitalized.

How did the boy fare so well despite spending a night in freezing temperatures? His father had enough forethought to warn his son what to do if he became lost, and his son had enough trust to do exactly as his father said.

Dominic protected himself from frostbite and hypothermia by snuggling up to a tree and covering himself with branches. He never would have known these survival techniques on his own, but he was simply obeying his wise and loving father.

Dominic's trusting obedience reminds me of how we Christians should respond to our loving and infinitely wise heavenly Father, who always knows what is best for us. Instead of following our natural impulses to walk according to this sin-filled world, we should follow our Father and obey His commands, which are clearly presented in the Bible.

The Apostle Peter tells us: "As obedient children, do not conform to the evil desires you had when you lived in ignorance. But just as he who called you is holy, so be holy in all you do; for it is written: 'Be holy, because I am holy'" (1 Peter 1:14-16).

Because our Father is holy, and because in Christ we have a holy standing before God, Scripture exhorts us to be holy in all that we do. Every time we sin, we are ignoring God's command to be holy. True, we can find forgiveness from our Father when we sin (1 John 1:9; 2:1-2); but sin is not to be the trademark of our lives.

Do you believe God knows what's best for you in this world filled with deceptive detours and confusing paths? Then trust your Father, and do exactly as He has said.

▼

Session Four:
Being Obedient

THE GOAL

Following Christ means we must obey Him day by day. Sometimes obeying Him isn't easy, but you'll find it is very rewarding. Ongoing peace, joy, fellowship, and much more are ours as we faithfully follow Him.

AT THE GROUP

Share

Share with other group members one verse from Luke's Gospel that you have found especially helpful. Explain how God has spoken to you about some area of your life.

Read

Do a careful, prayerful reading of Luke 5:1-11.

Think

(1) Complete the following statement for yourself: "If I had been Peter, my reaction would have been one of amazement, excitement, unworthiness, irritation, confusion, or_____."

(2) I think Jesus did this miracle to:
       help Peter become a great leader.
       help him to trust God more.
       make him feel unworthy.
       help him to obey Jesus even when he didn't understand.
       show him that being obedient brings rewards.
       _____(write your own).

(3) Catching men involves:
       telling them about Jesus.
       showing love and concern for them.
       helping to meet any needs they have.
       _____(write your own).

(4) What does being "catchers of men" involve today?

(5) Write one way in which you believe God wants you to obey Him
       this week. _____

       _____

Pray

Talk to God silently about all this. Reaffirm your desire to be Christ's
disciple, to follow Him, and to learn more about His plans for your life.

DURING THE WEEK

Each day remind yourself of specific ways you will *obey* God this
week.

       Pray that Jesus will help you obey Him in the above areas.

       Read Luke 24:36-53 in preparation for next week's study.

The Greatest Thrill

For a Christian, nothing can equal the excitement of helping some-
one else receive Jesus Christ. You, too, can tell others how your rela-
tionship with Jesus changed your life.

As a young man, I was convinced I didn't have the gift of evangelism. I was excited about preaching the Gospel of Jesus Christ at
evangelistic meetings. I prayed, studied, and preached, but no matter how hard I tried, no one was coming to faith in Jesus Christ.

I remember giving God a deadline: "If I don't see any converts by
the end of the year, I'm quitting." I would still be an active Christian,
but would resign myself to teaching other believers.

The end of the year came and went. No converts. Now I was sure
I didn't have the gift of evangelism.

About four days into the new year, I attended a home Bible study.
The fellow who was supposed to speak never showed up. So the man
of the house said, "Luis, you must say something." Unprepared, I read
Matthew 5:1-12 and simply repeated whatever I remembered from a
Billy Graham book I'd recently read.

As I was commenting on the beatitude "Blessed are the pure in heart, for they will see God," a woman suddenly stood up. She began to cry: "My heart is not pure. How can I see God? Somebody tell me how I can get a pure heart."

Before the evening was over, that woman found peace with God and went home with a pure heart overflowing with joy. How delightful it was to lead her to Jesus!

When you win someone to Christ, it's the greatest joy. Your graduation is exciting, your wedding day is exciting, your first baby is exciting. But the most thrilling thing you can ever do is win someone to Christ. Once you do it, you won't want to stop.

Yet today, in an effort to be sophisticated and contemporary, many Christians have stopped trying to persuade others to follow Christ. We don't want to offend people or appear strange. So we do nothing.

I, too, have been guilty of this. When I lived in Mexico City, my next-door neighbor was a young television personality. We would chat from time to time, but I didn't share the Gospel with him. *After all*, I thought, *he seems immune to the problems of life.*

Eventually, though, my neighbor changed. The joy seemed to have left his face. I could tell his marriage was souring, and I felt the need to talk with him, but I didn't want to meddle. I went about my business and headed off for an evangelistic crusade in Peru.

When I returned home, I learned my neighbor had killed himself. I was heartbroken. I knew I should have gone to him and persuaded him to repent and follow Christ. But because of false courtesy— because I followed a social norm—I didn't do it.

It's very convenient to make excuses for not persuading others to follow Christ. We may say we don't want to be overbearing or offensive. We may think we can't possibly witness to someone because he or she will become angry. But over the years I have learned that some of the people I thought would be most closed to the Gospel often are the most receptive. And having a part in leading that person to faith in Jesus Christ is exciting.

I challenge you to pray: "Dear God, I want that experience. I want to know what it is to win someone to Jesus Christ."

Why be ashamed of the Gospel? "It is the power of God for the salvation of everyone who believes" (Romans 1:16). It changes lives here and now and for eternity!

The Dutch evangelist Corrie ten Boom had a God-given desire to win others to Christ. One of her poems says:

> *When I enter that beautiful city*
> *And the saints all around me appear,*
> *I hope that someone will tell me:*
> *"It was you who invited me here."*

Whatever our place in the Body of Christ, let's actively and prayerfully invite others into God's kingdom. After all, God doesn't have a plan A, a plan B, and a plan C for evangelizing the world. He has only one plan—and that's you and me.

▼

Session Five:
Being Established

THE GOAL

As you grow in your faith, it is important that you learn to apply the Bible to your daily life, to pray for your family and friends, and to tell others about Christ and what He means to you.

AT THE GROUP

Look Back

Tell the group how you received God's strength as you tried to obey Him during the week.

Read

Do a careful, prayerful reading of Luke 24:36-53.

When a word or phrase strikes you in some way, mark it with one of these symbols:

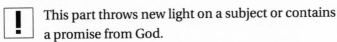 This part throws new light on a subject or contains a promise from God.

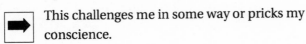 This challenges me in some way or pricks my conscience.

I do not understand this word, phrase, or verse, or I do not agree with it.

Share

Tell the group which passages you marked and why you marked them. This is one helpful method of group Bible study. You may want to try this method with other passages as well.

Think

Are there any particular people with whom you would like to share your experience of coming to know Christ and walking with Him? What are the problems you face in sharing Christ with these people? How can some of these difficulties be overcome?

Pray

Pray for the person on your left, remembering specific needs that may have arisen during the Bible study or sharing time. When you are part of a group it is helpful to pray aloud, but you may pray silently if you prefer. During times of silence when no one else is praying, share your thoughts with God; but listen when others are praying aloud.

DURING THE WEEK

Pray for the people with whom you want to share your faith. Expect God to give you opportunities to talk to them.

Read Luke 12:4-12 in preparation for next week's study.

How to Study the Bible

Now that you have committed your life to Jesus Christ, you should take time every day to study the Bible and to learn to apply biblical truths to your life. To grow and mature spiritually, we must regularly study God's Word.

Here are three simple steps to successful Bible study.

OBSERVATION

Bible study begins with observation. We observe the Bible by carefully reading it daily. Noted Bible teacher Dr. James M. Gray said, "There is only one law of Bible study, and that is to read the Book, and when you have read it, to read it again, and then sit down and read it again, and then sit down and read it once more, and by and by you will come to know the Book."

Once a person knows Christ as personal Savior, Philippians (or perhaps James) is a good book to study at first. Read the entire book in one sitting in order to get a clear impression of the book as a whole. Disregard chapter and verse divisions. Read it again and again, occasionally using different translations to better grasp its message. Ask probing questions: Who? What? When? Where? Why? How?

INTERPRETATION

Pray for the Holy Spirit to give you understanding as you interpret the Scriptures, for apart from His illumination, proper understanding is impossible (see 1 John 2:20, 27). Examine the context of the passage you are interpreting. Consider the verses before and after the section being read, and compare it with parallel accounts.

The nineteenth-century evangelist Charles Spurgeon said, "Nowadays we hear men tear a simple sentence of Scripture from its connection and cry, 'Eureka! Eureka!' as if they had found a new truth; and yet they have not found a truth diamond, but a piece of broken glass."

Although the best Bible commentary is the Bible itself, it can be helpful occasionally to consult Bible handbooks, dictionaries, and a good atlas to better understand biblical lands, customs, and history. But don't spend too much time reading about the Bible without reading God's Word for yourself.

APPLICATION

As you seek to apply God's Word to your life, you'll find your behavior changing. Relate the Bible to all areas of your life—your strengths and weaknesses, your attitudes and actions. What does Scripture say to you as a parent or child, employee or employer?

James 1:22 tells us: "Do not merely listen to the word, and so deceive yourselves. Do what it says." Obey the Word by prayerfully meditating on it with the goal of better understanding and applying it.

Observation. Interpretation. Application. These simple steps are the keys that open the door for exciting, life-changing Bible study.

Memorizing God's Word

Warning: Authorities have determined that Scripture memorization may be hazardous to your spiritual health.

Dawson Trotman, founder of The Navigators, once asked a young man how much Scripture he knew. The serviceman said he had memorized 1,500 verses.

"You mean you could quote 1,500 verses to me right now?" Trotman asked incredulously.

"That's right," the young man said with obvious pride.

Trotman replied, "I wish you could quote only five verses but *live* them!" This young man had only head knowledge of Scripture, not heart application.

Many years ago the village priest in Kalonovaka, Russia, took a special liking to a pug-nosed lad who recited his Scriptures with proper piety. By offering various inducements, the priest managed to teach the boy the four Gospels, which he recited nonstop in church one day.

Sixty years later he still liked to recite Scriptures, but in a context that would have horrified the old priest. The prize pupil who memorized so much of the Bible was Nikita Khrushchev, later to become premier of the Soviet Union!

John W. Alexander, former president of InterVarsity Christian Fellowship, gives us this warning: "There is little merit inherent in the mere process of memorizing Scripture. One could memorize voluminous portions and be an atheist. Satan memorized enough to use it to tempt Jesus."

Alexander goes on to add, however, "Memorizing *is* helpful when we yearn for Scripture to energize our whole lives."

Warning: Authorities also have determined that Scripture memorization can greatly enhance your spiritual vitality.

What makes the difference between superficial and beneficial Scripture memorization? I believe it is *prayerful meditation.*

Memorization in itself may sharpen our intellectual capacities, but that's about all. Memorization with a view to meditation helps us think straight in a crooked world.

The Bible says, "Whatever is true, whatever is noble, whatever is right, whatever is pure, whatever is lovely, whatever is admirable—if anything is excellent or praiseworthy—think about such things" (Philippians 4:8).

How can we think on what is pure when we are confronted daily with impurity? By purposefully meditating on God's Word.

We can't read the Bible all day, but we can always meditate on passages of Scripture—if we have memorized them. After twenty-four hours, research shows, we accurately remember 5 percent of what we heard, 15 percent of what we read, 35 percent of what we studied, but 100 percent of what we have memorized.

Let me suggest five tips for memorizing Scripture that I think you will find helpful.

(1) Read the verse out loud at least ten times.

(2) Write it out on an index card, thinking about each word.

(3) Practice quoting it (it should be easy by now).

(4) Meditate on it throughout the day, and review it on subsequent days.

(5) Share the verse with other people as you converse together.

I strongly encourage you to start memorizing Scripture passages and meditating on them. But let me warn you: It may change your life!

Scripture Passages That Have Changed My Life

Approaching Scripture with an open heart affects our lives from top to bottom! If we want to follow Christ faithfully, it is imperative that we spend time in God's Word—hearing it, reading it, studying it, thinking about it, memorizing it. Memorization helps plant the truths of the Bible in our hearts, so that when we face situations when we need the Word *now*, we'll have it.

If you don't have an established Scripture memorization plan, start with the verses I have listed below. I have memorized and meditated on all these passages, and they have made a significant difference in my life. They can change your life too.

NEW BIRTH

Salvation—John 3:16.
New life—2 Corinthians 5:17.
Becoming like children—Luke 18:17.
Our identity as God's children—1 John 3:1-2.
God lives in you—1 Corinthians 6:19-20.
All believers baptized into one body—1 Corinthians 12:13.

GOD

Christ as the Word—John 1:1-2.
The Spirit of God—John 15:26.
The Counselor—John 14:16-17.
God's strength given to us—Ephesians 6:10-11.

FAMILY

Wives—Ephesians 5:22.
Husbands—Ephesians 5:25.
Children—Ephesians 6:1-3.
Parents—Ephesians 6:4.

GROWTH

Temptation—1 Corinthians 10:13.
Confession and forgiveness—1 John 1:9.
Prayer—Luke 11:9-10; John 14:13-14.
Living for Christ—Luke 9:23-24.
Meeting together—Hebrews 10:24-25.
Loving one another—John 13:34-35.
Loving your enemies—Luke 6:35.
Freedom from legalism (serving rules rather than Christ)—
Colossians 2:20-22.

GOD'S WORD

Its authority—2 Peter 1:20-21.
Its purpose—2 Timothy 3:16-17.
Given for our purity—Psalm 119:9-11.

VICTORY

Walking in the Spirit—Galatians 5:16-18.
Dedication and transformation—Romans 12:1-2.
Faith—Luke 17:6.

Victory through the cross—Galatians 2:20.

Overcoming obstacles—Luke 1:37.

The fruit of the Spirit—Galatians 5:22-23.

The Great Commission—Matthew 28:18-20.

Death and resurrection in Christ—Romans 6:3-4.

THE FUTURE

Eternal condemnation—Revelation 21:8.

Heaven—John 14:1-3.

Discipline yourself to learn one verse or short passage each week. Check off each verse as you learn it. Start small: (re)memorize John 3:16 this week. Next week, (re)learn 2 Corinthians 5:17. Get into the habit of reviewing the Scripture verses you already know.

But don't stop there! Meditate on these verses. Say them over in your mind occasionally throughout the day. Keep asking, "What difference should this make in my life?"

Pray that you will keep each verse not only in your head, but also in your heart, so that God can use it to change your life (Psalm 119:11). Ask God to help you hear what He is trying to say to you through His Word.

▼

Session Six:
Continuing

THE GOAL

You have probably already discovered that the Christian life is some-times difficult. During this session you will learn how God's Holy Spirit helps us through difficult times and how you can learn to trust Him more.

AT THE GROUP

Share

Tell the group what you have enjoyed most about these meetings and the area of your life where you are most aware of growth.

Read

Do a careful, prayerful reading of Luke 12:4-12.

(1) What does this passage warn Christians to expect as they live in obedience to Jesus Christ?

(2) In what ways do we experience this today? Give some specific examples.

(3) What comfort does Jesus offer to His followers in these situations?

(4) How does this help us in relation to the examples in question 2?

Think

What specific action can you take to enable you to continue to grow as a Christian? Share your plans in groups of two or three. Help one another to see the potential benefits and problems of these plans.

Pray

In your group of two or three, pray that God would help each of you grow as Christians.

THE NEXT STEP

On Your Own

We've seen that the Christian life isn't always easy. We need to seek God's strength daily through prayer and Bible reading. A variety of Christian resources is available to help you in your quest for Christian maturity. Check Part V of this book for a list of helpful Christian books. Also ask your group leader or pastor to suggest other excellent Christian resources.

In a Group

You have discovered how helpful it is to learn in a group setting. Consider joining a permanent Bible study or other group in your church. Ask your group leader or pastor for more information.

In Your Church

When you became a Christian, you also became part of God's family. Meeting regularly with other Christians in the church for worship, prayer, and teaching helps us grow. We should accept our role along with the rest of the church in discovering God's will for our lives and for living for Him in our community.

Getting Your Roots Deep into the Local Church

Now that you have decided to follow Jesus Christ, how will you continue to mature in your Christian life? The best catalyst for Christian growth is to get your roots deep into the local church.

Many Christians don't recognize the importance of getting involved in a local church. They have good excuses. Spending time with their family comes first. Or perhaps they attend several Bible studies, but can't seem to find the "right" church. Others listen to sermons on the radio or television instead. All of these are worthwhile activities, but we must not substitute any of them for the local church.

The Bible clearly states the importance of the local church:

> And let us consider how we may spur one another on toward love and good deeds. Let us not give up meeting together, as some are in the habit of doing, but let us encourage one another—and all the more as you see the Day approaching.
> —Hebrews 10:24-25

If you neglect the local church, you lose. Perhaps you have family, health, and financial responsibilities and a busy schedule;

maybe you think you don't need Christian friends. But when the storms of life hit—and they will—you'll have no Christian friends to support you.

How can you get your roots deep into the local church?

Make a commitment to your local church by attending regularly. Follow the appropriate procedures to become a member. Tell the pastor you would like to be baptized and thus publicly identify yourself as a believer in the Lord Jesus Christ. Let the leaders know you want to be an active part of the church and submit to their authority.

Speak well of your church. Even though it has faults, don't allow yourself to develop a critical spirit (1 Corinthians 1:10). When others grumble about the church, remind them that they should take major concerns to the elders and not gossip to the rest of the body.

Your church is your family in Christ. Defend it. Parents should speak well of "our church," "our pastor," and "our Sunday school class." This will help your children claim the church as their own.

You can also speak well of your church by inviting others to attend with you. One church historian found that the average person in a certain denomination invites others to church only once every twenty-eight years. Surely you can do better than that!

Seek to minister within your local church. You'll find many opportunities for ministry—even for the beginning Christian. Sing in the choir. Supervise children in the nursery. Offer to drive an elderly member to church. Pray daily for the pastor. Type the church bulletin. Sweep the walkway. Invite your neighbors to attend church with you. Endless opportunities to serve await you in your local church.

Financially support your local church. Although the New Testament doesn't state a fixed percentage that we should give, it does emphasize the importance of giving regularly. In 2 Corinthians the Apostle Paul explains that we should give proportionately (8:12), generously (9:6), purposefully (9:7), and cheerfully (9:7). Some Christians will be able to give more than others, but the amount we give isn't what impresses the Lord. He looks at our motives for giving and the sacrifices we make in order to give.

Show hospitality to your church's missionaries. Invite them home for dinner. Your children will fall more in love with the Lord because missionaries who were on fire for God spent time in your home.

Sink your roots deep into the local church. Serve Christ there abundantly and faithfully and fervently. This will help you keep growing spiritually and will encourage you in your new life with Christ.

The God
Of All Life

Faith:
Experiencing
God's Forgiveness

Billy Staton slipped a recording device into his shirt before going to pick up his daughter for a picnic, planning to tape his ex-wife's hostility about his visitation rights.

Instead, Staton recorded his own slaying in what one prosecutor called "twenty-three minutes of murder." Paul Wolf, twenty-one, was charged with Staton's death. According to the state prosecutors, the tape conclusively proved that Wolf committed the brutal murder. But the Associated Press reported that he pleaded innocent to the slaying.

Wolf's attorney told the jurors that his client was innocent because he was "legally insane" the day of the killing. He explained that Wolf had had a difficult childhood, then faced an ongoing series of custody problems after his marriage to Staton's ex-wife.

The attorney explained that Wolf did not plan the killing, but was *forced* to bludgeon twenty-six-year-old Staton to death "at the last minute after the steady, lengthy, continual buildup of the pressure."

Are you surprised when you read about people making excuses for criminal actions? Probably not. It's almost expected these days. Admitting one's guilt has become passé. Instead, our society works double-time trying to cover up personal responsibility with carefully constructed explanations for wrongdoing.

In *Newsweek* psychologist Rex Julian Beaber pointed out:

> The new "sciences" of sociology, psychology, and psychiatry have cast aside such concepts as will, will power, badness, and laziness and replaced them with political and psychological repression, poor conditioning, diseased family interaction, and bad genes. One by one, human failings have been redesignated as diseases.

Beaber counters this modern trend by stating: "The American lust for scientific sounding explanations is completely out of control. . . . Ultimately, we must assume responsibility for our actions."

Sin needs to be rediscovered once more in our generation.

The Apostle John spells this out clearly: "If we claim to be without sin, we deceive ourselves and the truth is not in us" (1 John 1:8). The deadliest sin is assuming we have none.

THE WRONG RESPONSE

Christians and non-Christians alike often make excuses for their failures, deny their wrongdoing, or pretend their guilt feelings don't exist. But God calls us to seek, to know, and to experience His forgiveness and cleansing.

It's not enough to regret our mistakes, to say, "I'm sorry," and seek to justify our actions. Regretting the consequences of our actions belies the seriousness of our sin and our responsibility.

Nor will remorse for our sin get rid of our burden of guilt. The dictionary defines remorse as "a gnawing distress arising from a sense of guilt for past actions." And it will eat you alive.

THE CORRECT RESPONSE

Repentance is the biblical, correct response to sin. The moment we committed our life to Christ, all our sins—past, present, and future—

were forgiven. God's righteousness was satisfied. But now as children of God we must maintain fellowship with God by confessing our sins to our heavenly Father as we become aware of them.

Once we let go of guilt and properly deal with our sins, we are free to revel in God's mercy. The beauty of Scripture is its good news that God freely and willingly bestows mercy on anyone who honestly confesses his sins to Him. We needn't fear finding God in an unforgiving mood. He loves to pardon sinners and to cleanse His people!

God promises, "Their sins and lawless acts I will remember no more" (Hebrews 10:17). How remarkable it is that the omniscient Lord of the universe promises not only to forgive our sins, but also to forget them forever!

CONFESSING OUR SINS TO OTHERS

Even after God forgives our sins and forgets them forever, our past isn't magically erased. Hurt and angry people still lie along the way behind us. With God's help we must go back to each one we can find and ask for his or her forgiveness.

I want to suggest a project that will help you settle the things of the past. Make a list of people you've hurt, things you need to set right. After you have made your list, lay it down before the Lord. (No one else needs to see it, so destroy it as soon as you can.) Confess your sins to Him. Then determine how you will contact each person on your list to ask for his or her forgiveness and make restitution, if necessary.

The Bible says, "Confess your sins to each other and pray for each other so that you may be healed" (James 5:16). Confession is the healing balm of our soul.

FORGIVING OTHERS

But what do we do when others wrong us? What do we do when someone takes advantage of us? When someone walks out of our life?

The story of Joseph, one of my favorite Bible characters, is instructive. (You can read about him in Genesis 37–50.)

The Bible gives us many reasons why Joseph could have been a very bitter man. Not only had his brothers hated him and sold him into slavery, but his master's wife falsely accused him of a serious crime and had him thrown into an Egyptian prison. Later a government official promised to try to secure Joseph's release but left him there to rot. Despite all these things, Joseph did not allow any root of bitterness to take hold in his life (compare Hebrews 12:15). Joseph followed the principle quoted here and repeated over and over in the Bible: "Bear with each other and forgive whatever grievances you may have against one another. Forgive as the Lord forgave you" (Colossians 3:13). Unfortunately, that can't be said of everyone.

I believe more lives are spoiled by bitterness and a lack of forgiveness than anything else. And the longer we carry a grudge, the heavier it becomes. We cannot afford to harbor bitterness in our soul. The price we must pay is too great!

KEEPING SHORT ACCOUNTS

Forgive and be forgiven. And then forget it! This is the secret of spiritual health. Keep short accounts with God and men (Acts 24:16). Don't lock bitterness and guilt within some closet of your soul!

Allow the Holy Spirit to shine His divine spotlight in your heart. Let Him clean out every closet. Allow Him to free you from the bitterness you may feel toward someone else or the guilt you may feel within yourself.

Then claim God's wonderful promise: "If we confess our sins, he is faithful and just and will forgive us our sins and purify us from all unrighteousness" (1 John 1:9).

May you experience His cleansing and healing today!

▼

Faith:
Living as a
Christian

"I wonder why it is," a British church leader once asked aloud, "that everywhere the Apostle Paul went they had a revolution and everywhere I go they serve a cup of tea?"

Today we live such a relatively easy life. But the Apostle Paul could hardly set foot in a city before a riot started. It seemed like Paul was always getting into trouble (see the book of Acts)!

Why was Paul such a controversial yet effective Christian leader in his day? Because he knew the secret of living like a man sent from God. He reveals his secret in 2 Corinthians 2:14-17.

PAUL'S THANKFUL ATTITUDE

> But thanks be to God, who always leads us in triumphal procession in Christ.
>
> —2 Corinthians 2:14

Despite his intense hardships and sufferings, Paul consistently maintained an attitude of thankfulness and joy. When he was thrown into prison, what did he do? Grumble and complain? No! He sang hymns of joy to God (Acts 16:25). Imprisoned a second time, he encouraged others to "rejoice in the Lord always" (Philippians 4:4). Paul's dominant attitude—whatever his circumstance—was *joy*.

When we make happiness the goal of our lives, we can't find it or keep it. But when we make following Christ and abiding in Him the main thing in our lives, we will find true joy.

Because Paul knew God was at work in his life, he maintained a thankful attitude—even in the midst of difficulties.

PAUL'S TRIUMPHANT ACTIONS

Someone once asked William Booth about the secret of his success. He thought for a moment, and then tears welled up in his eyes. "I will tell you the secret," he said. "God has all there was of me to have. . . . If there is anything of power in the Salvation Army today, it is because God has had all the adoration of my heart, all the power of my will, and all the influence of my life."

We can live victoriously as men and women sent from God only as we abide in Him and He abides in us. Only then we can bear much fruit, for apart from Him we can do nothing (John 15:5).

PAUL'S FRAGRANT INFLUENCE

> . . . and through us spreads everywhere the fragrance of the knowledge of him. For we are to God the aroma of Christ among those who are being saved and those who are perishing.
>
> —2 Corinthians 2:14-15

Wherever Paul went he influenced people. Either they loved him or they hated him. But they couldn't ignore him—or his God. The fragrance of his living in the power of the indwelling Christ permeated the air around him.

The fragrance of Christ cannot be imitated. You cannot fabricate it, masquerade it, or work it up through self-effort. Has anything come between you and the Lord? Confess your sins and walk transparently. Don't worry about impressing others. Walk honestly and openly among men.

PAUL'S FAULTLESS INTEGRITY

Unlike so many, we do not peddle the word of God for profit. On the contrary, in Christ we speak before God with sincerity, like men sent from God.

—2 Corinthians 2:14-17

In all of his dealings with others, Paul sought to maintain unquestionable integrity.

Some may go through all the outward motions of being sincere Christians, but they are only sincere hypocrites. They try to talk like Spirit-filled Christians, but they know nothing of living in the power of the indwelling Christ. Perhaps we ourselves are doing that.

What we need to do at such times is to take off our masks and stop the show. The world is waiting to hear men and women who are honestly thankful—whatever their circumstances. The world is longing to see men and women who act victoriously in the power of the indwelling Christ. The world is yearning to sense the fragrance of Christ upon men and women around them. People are waiting to meet a Christian who has taken off his or her mask and lives what he or she believes—a Christian sent from God to a world in need.

Family: Do You Want a Happy Home?

Many people today are searching for solutions to the heartaches plaguing homes today. We all want a happy home. I've never heard anyone say he or she got married to be unhappy. Still, many families experience unhappiness.

The secret of a happy home—if it can be called a secret—is in the Bible, the most marvelous book of all time.

The Bible teaches us that the Christian marriage is a triangle—made up of three people, not just two. The third person is Jesus Christ. When Christ is in the heart of the man and the woman, the foundation for a happy home has been laid. And when we follow the principles He has laid out in His Word, we can have a happy home.

HUSBAND, RECOGNIZE YOUR PART

The Bible says something amazing to husbands: "For the husband is the head of the wife as Christ is the head of the church, his body, of which he is the Savior" (Ephesians 5:23).

This means the husband symbolizes Christ to the family. He is the head of the home. What does it mean to be "the head" and a symbol of Christ?

First, it means that the *husband must love in a sacrificial way.* The Bible says, "Husbands, love your wives, just as Christ loved the church and gave himself up for her" (Ephesians 5:25).

In a happy home, the husband sacrificially loves his wife week after week, month after month, year after year. As time passes, he loves her deeper and deeper and shows his love through his actions.

Second, *the loving husband supports and cares for his wife.* "After all, no one ever hated his own body, but he feeds and cares for it, just as Christ does the church" (Ephesians 5:29-30).

A husband must take care of his wife just as he does his own body. Part of taking care of your wife includes supporting her materially and financially. You have the responsibility to provide for the needs of the home and to take care of your wife with all the passion and strength of your being.

Another aspect of caring for your wife is working to understand her, then acting according to what you have learned. If your wife likes flowers, surprise her with a dozen roses. Treat her with courtesy. Hold her hand as you walk down the street.

Finally, *the husband who loves his wife lives with her in a holy and honorable way.* The Bible says husbands are to be completely free from sexual immorality. "For God did not call us to be impure, but to live a holy life" (1 Thessalonians 4:7). A husband must have mastery over himself and not be controlled by lustful desires.

THE WOMAN'S ROLE

God also has given principles for women to follow.

First, *the Bible tells the wife that she must respect her husband* (Ephesians 5:33). Respect has to do with the attitude of the heart. Not only is this an outward demonstration, but also an internal appreciation. With a respect filled with affection, the wife should encourage her husband and show him love.

Second, *the Bible says, "wives must submit to your husbands as to the Lord.* For the husband is the head of the wife as Christ is the head of the church, his body, of which he is the Savior" (Ephesians 5:22-23).

Because the husband has been designated by God to be the head of the home, the wife is subject to him. Your husband is responsible for making the decisions of the home, for discipline of children, and for the spiritual life of the family. That's not to say you can't share your thoughts with your husband and offer advice. However, you should submit to your husband's decision as though submitting to the Lord.

And finally, *the Bible teaches that the wife must be pure.* "[Let them] see the purity and reverence of your lives" (1 Peter 3:2).

Secret and improper desires must be cut off. Purity is not fabricated, but is produced by Christ in one's heart. It reveals itself in words, looks, dress, and actions. The woman who desires a happy home does not flirt with other men because she has dedicated herself to her husband.

FORGIVING EACH OTHER DAILY

What a wonderful fragrance there is to the words, "Please forgive me for what I've done wrong." If you want happiness to last in your family, you will have to forgive your spouse many times.

Scripture says, "Be kind and compassionate to one another, forgiving each other, just as in Christ God forgave you" (Ephesians 4:32). God has forgiven our many sins through Christ. As we remember how much God has forgiven us, it's much easier to forgive others.

AN UNBELIEVING SPOUSE

Many spouses have asked me, "Mr. Palau, my husband (or wife) does not want to believe in Christ. What should I do?" The best answer is found in the Bible:

Wives, in the same way be submissive to your husbands so that, if any of them do not believe the word, they may be won over without talk by the behavior of their wives, when they see the purity and reverence of your lives.

—1 Peter 3:1-2

The Apostle Paul gives this counsel:

To the rest I say this (I, not the Lord): If any brother has a wife who is not a believer and she is willing to live with him, he must not divorce her. And if a woman has a husband who is not a believer and he is willing to live with her, she must not divorce him. For the unbelieving husband has been sanctified through his wife, and the unbelieving wife has been sanctified through her believing husband.

—1 Corinthians 7:12-14

How valuable is the example of a spouse whose life is controlled by Christ!

THE SECRET: CHRIST IN YOUR HEART

Jesus Christ is the secret of happiness. He must be in the heart of each member of the family. He must be the Lord of daily life. With Christ in our hearts, the home is a taste of heaven on earth.

Still, all families—even Christian ones—have struggles and times of difficulty. No one is free from problems—economic difficulties, unemployment, the death of a loved one, unpleasant decisions. We must remember the words of the Lord Jesus, who warned His disciples:

"I have told you these things, so that in me you may have peace. In this world you will have trouble. But take heart! I have overcome the world."

—John 16:33

A happy, harmonious family will not happen instantly. We must seek and work for the happiness of our marriage and family. We must spend time with our family. A happy family is the result of a couple's dedication to pursue Christ. Work determinedly, take responsibility, put Christ in the center of your life, and soon you will see results.

May God bless your home today and forever!

Family:
How to Lead Your
Child to Christ

The Lord longs to welcome children into His family. "Let the little children come to me," Jesus said, "and do not hinder them, for the kingdom of heaven belongs to such as these" (Matthew 19:14). Through our prayers and encouragement, we can have an active part in leading our sons and daughters to faith in Christ.

Leading your child to Jesus Christ may not happen all in one day, of course. As parents, we may have the privilege of introducing the Lord to our children over a period of several years. There's so much to talk about and discover together.

TELLING THE GOSPEL STORY

One of the most important ways we can communicate our faith to our children is by leading them in family worship. Time for Bible reading, memorization, discussion, prayer, and singing should be a natural, enjoyable, and daily part of family life.

God has designed the home as the place where His Word is to be taught, lived, and passed on from generation to generation. Deuteronomy 6:6-7 says, "These commandments that I give you today are to be upon your hearts. Impress them on your children. Talk about them when you sit at home and when you walk along the road, when you lie down and when you get up."

The influence of a godly parent cannot be overestimated. It's in the home where life's most crucial curriculum is taught. Children may spend 1 percent of their time in church, 16 percent in school, but much of the remaining 83 percent in and around the home.

Columbia University in New York spent about $250,000 on a research project only to discover a biblical truth: there is no second force in a child's life compared to the impact of the home.

COVERING THE BASICS

Our emphasis in presenting the Gospel to our children should be that God is our heavenly Father. That is essential. Instead of initially focusing on sin—"We hurt the Lord when we do wrong things"—we should major on the fact that our heavenly Father, who is perfect, loves us with an everlasting love. But the issue of sin also needs to be addressed.

To experience God's love, our children must own up to those things in their lives that hurt Him—selfishness, pride, deceit, and all the rest. They need to see that "the wages of sin is death" (Romans 6:23). They need to learn that "all have sinned and fall short of the glory of God" (Romans 3:23). That includes everyone, young and old alike.

Your child may not completely understand how God places the penalty for his or her sin on His Son. That's okay. God simply asks us to respond to Him based on what we do know.

LEADING IN A PRAYER OF COMMITMENT

If your son or daughter asks, "Well, how do I become a Christian?" turn to Scripture for the answer. We like to use Romans 10:9-10 with children, inserting their names in the blanks. "If you, _____, confess with your mouth, 'Jesus is Lord,' and believe in your heart that God raised him from the dead, you, _____, will be saved. For it is with your heart that you, _____, believe and are justified, and it is with your mouth that you, _____, confess and are saved."

The best way we know for an individual to make Jesus the Lord of his or her life is to bow his or her head in prayer, confess his or her sins to God, by faith open his or her heart to Christ, believe in Him, and receive Him.

Pray together with your child, and after you finish praying together, ask several questions to help your child clarify the decision he or she just made. Then celebrate that decision! Give your child opportunities to share the joy of his or her decision with family members and Christian friends.

To help your child look back on that decision, encourage him or her to write it down in a Bible or New Testament.

THE NEED FOR ASSURANCE

As a parent, we should not say anything immediately if we hear a child make the statement, "I asked Jesus into my heart again today." Wait for a good, teachable moment when the subject comes up naturally and then say, "When we come to Jesus, we belong to Him forever. Nothing can separate us from God's love."

Lack of assurance is a sign of immaturity. Children need reassurance. Parents can move alongside a child and say, "Aren't you glad that Jesus will never, ever let you out of His hands? He's never going to let you go. You're part of His family forever." It's also helpful to memorize biblical promises about assurance, such as John 10:28, with a child. That's where we need to go when doubts come.

DISCIPLESHIP IN THE HOME

Our goal as Christian parents is to lead our children into a personal relationship with the Lord Jesus Christ and then spend the rest of their childhood years discipling them. We need to keep those two concepts separate in our thinking. First we're born into God's family; then the lifelong process of discipleship begins.

As parents, we often see things in our children's lives that are inconsistent with Christianity, and we sometimes fail to handle the situation with care. In the home, where we have the privilege of saying anything that crosses our mind, our worst side often comes out. But it's helpful when you're looking at your child and wondering "Is this kid really a Christian?" to remember when *we* were born again. We didn't grow up in Christ overnight. We need to have long memories.

In Philippians 1:6, Paul speaks of "being confident of this, that he who began a good work in you will carry it on to completion until the day of Christ Jesus." Every Christian can enjoy this same confidence. As soon as a child accepts Jesus Christ as Savior, he or she is saved. God has begun a good work in that child's life, even if we can't always see it.

Tragically, some people resist the idea of evangelizing children. In our evangelistic campaigns in Europe, we've seen men and women holding back their children from going forward to confess the Lord Jesus as their Savior. We're seeing that trend in America now, too.

Other parents don't talk about the issue of salvation with their children, as if it were just a theological matter for adults to discuss at church. The message many children are picking up is: "Wait until you grow up and then you can make your decision." But it's really the other way around.

Unless we become like little children, we can't enter the kingdom of heaven. "The kingdom of heaven belongs to such as these," said Jesus. Let's actively, prayerfully encourage our children to come to Him.

▼

Personal Growth: Experiencing Personal Renewal

If you were to consider the desires, motives, thoughts, and actions of most Christians, I think you would discover that all growing believers want the same thing: they desire to live in the presence of God, they long to communicate Jesus Christ in a powerful way, and they seek daily spiritual renewal.

The spiritual renewal we long for is a result of the life of Jesus at work within us, flowing through us day after day. How can this life be appropriated? The answer is found in the following verses:

> But we have this treasure in jars of clay to show that this all-surpassing power is from God and not from us. We are hard pressed on every side, but not crushed; perplexed, but not in despair; persecuted, but not abandoned; struck down, but not destroyed. We always carry around in our body the death of Jesus, so that the life of Jesus may also be revealed in our body.
> —2 Corinthians 4:7-10

We Christians have a treasure within us—nothing less than God Himself! Paul says this marvelous treasure is contained in clay jars—our bodies. Our bodies are so fragile. We have to treat them with great care. Yet God has chosen to dwell within our humble, imperfect human bodies. In our bodies dwell the power and the glory of the resurrected Christ!

SUSTAINING INNER RENEWAL

If the power of the living Christ is in every believer, why isn't it always visible? Why do we sometimes feel defeated, depressed, frustrated, and fruitless?

Paul explains when he says, "We always carry around in our body the death of Jesus, so that the life of Jesus may also be revealed in our body" (2 Corinthians 4:10). The death of Jesus must be at work in us before we can see the results of the life of Christ. But how does the death of Jesus work in us? What does this mean in our daily lives?

Whenever we choose God's will over our own, the death of Jesus is at work in us. In the Garden of Gethsemane, Jesus provided a perfect example of choosing God's will over our own. Jesus was the perfect man. He knew God's will for His life and wanted it. Nevertheless, Jesus wasn't a masochist who couldn't wait to be beaten and mocked, who couldn't wait for the nails to be pounded through His hands. Jesus prayed that He wouldn't have to drink such a bitter cup. But Jesus knew the will of the Father and chose God's will over His own— not in resignation, but in a clear-cut, meaningful decision.

Jesus' choice is an example to all of us. Whenever we choose God's will over ours, we are dying to ego, pride, passion, and desire. When we choose God's will over our own, we become Christ-conscious instead of self-conscious, and the life of Jesus begins to flow through us. God then can use us to bring life to others because He is having His way in our lives.

SQUELCHING INNER RENEWAL

Sometimes we think the choices we have to make between our will and God's will are insignificant. We think, *Oh, this decision isn't that important. It won't matter if I choose my will instead of God's will this time.* But that is not the case. Every time we choose God's will over our own, the life of Jesus flows through us. When we choose our will instead of God's will, we are saddled with defeat, discouragement, and depression. We cannot be filled with the joy of the Spirit. We miss out on the opportunities and blessings God wants to bestow upon us. But if we confess our sins—if we confess the times we have chosen our will rather than God's—He will cleanse, purify, and use us.

LIVING IN DAILY RENEWAL

The power of the indwelling Christ is what keeps dynamic Christians excited about life. The preeminent characteristic of God's outstanding servants throughout church history is that, with few exceptions, they persistently served the Lord. John Wesley and Corrie ten Boom immediately come to mind. Both served God long after the age most people hope to retire. They weren't persistent out of their own stubbornness, like many unhappy Christians who strive to serve God out of their own ability. Rather, these servants persistently walked in the power of the indwelling Christ.

The older we are and the longer we walk with Christ, the more renewed and youthful we become. As Paul says, "Though outwardly we are wasting away, yet inwardly we are being renewed day by day" (2 Corinthians 4:16).

What a thrill! When we walk with Christ, our bodies may weaken and fall apart, but spiritually we are growing stronger every day. Can you imagine how "super-renewed" you will be after choosing God's will over your will for fifty, sixty, or seventy years? Your old body may fall apart, but the inner person is just beginning to show through.

Several years ago I sat next to Joy Ridderhof of Gospel Recordings at a fund-raising dinner. She had been a missionary in Latin America and talked to me at machine-gun pace, in Spanish, all through dinner. Though Joy was in her seventies at the time, she didn't talk about the old days. Instead, she talked about my ministry. She talked about how we could enhance our follow-up of new believers by giving them a recording of some of my messages on Christian growth.

I told her she had a good idea, but I didn't see how our team could afford to pay for such a venture. "Don't worry about the money, Luis," she replied. "Just record some messages and send them to me right away."

When I arrived home several days later, I received a letter from Joy reminding me that I needed to send her the messages. I did, and she provided our team with thousands of records to give to new Christians. When I'm in my seventies, that's the kind of vision and faith I want to have!

When we are renewed through Jesus Christ, the excitement never dies. We don't lose heart! The life of Jesus just flows stronger and stronger, renewing us more and more.

We are joyful and victorious because the Lord Jesus is alive and working within us. This is what Christianity is all about. It isn't a religion we follow—it's the life of Christ that fills us, making us new people.

Personal Growth: Speaking Well of God's Son

One cold, windy night two Christian youths headed toward the tavern district in their hometown of Glasgow, Scotland, with the "preposterous" idea of holding an open-air Gospel meeting. The two young men began singing hymns to gather a crowd. Their singing was tolerated, but whenever they stopped singing to share the saving message of Jesus Christ, they were mocked by the crowd with vulgar hoots and jeering howls.

Frederick S. Arnot and his friend were quite sincere about sharing their faith and the gospel message with the drunks along tavern row. Yet the crowd was determined not to let them talk. Finally Arnot, with tears running down his face, acknowledged defeat. He and his friend turned to leave.

Suddenly someone grabbed Arnot's shoulder. Startled, Arnot turned to find a tall, elderly man towering over him. The stranger smiled warmly and said quietly, "Keep at it, laddie. God loves to hear men speak well of His Son."

With that encouragement, the two Scottish lads squared their shoulders and returned. It wasn't long before the rowdy crowd began to pay attention to the message the young men wanted to share.

In 1881, several years after this incident, Arnot, influenced by the example set by David Livingstone, left his Scottish mission field and headed for Central Africa, where God used him in a great way to proclaim the Gospel.

God loves to hear men and women speak well of His Son. Yet it's so easy for us to become silent, ineffective ambassadors for Christ because of discouragement, lack of results, or some other excuse. Do you speak well of God's Son? Are you telling others about Him and His salvation? If not, what is your excuse?

In an honest and challenging article entitled "Excuses," seminary professor Norman L. Geisler admits that even though he was in full-time Christian ministry for eighteen years, he never witnessed for Christ. His excuses sound familiar, don't they?

> (1) "I didn't have the gift of evangelism. It was obvious to me that someone like Billy Graham did, and it was equally obvious that I didn't."
>
> (2) "I had the gift of teaching [Christians], and it's pretty hard to make converts from that group."
>
> (3) "I didn't like . . . impersonal evangelism, so I would do 'friendship evangelism.' I wasn't going to cram the Gospel down anybody's throat."
>
> (4) "I came to the conclusion that if God is sovereign . . . then He can do it with or without me."

One day, however, a visiting speaker demolished Geisler's excuses by saying, "I've been a missionary for years and I was never *called* . . . I was just *commanded* like the rest of you." That statement startled Geisler, and he became a fisher of men.

"Go into all the world and preach the good news to all creation" (Mark 16:15) wasn't a suggestion, but a command of the Lord Jesus

Christ. Perhaps you were once eager like Arnot to witness for Christ, but somehow that zeal has faded. Or perhaps you are just beginning to witness to those around you about your Savior. Just remember, God loves to hear you speak well of His Son.

▼

Personal Growth:
How to Pray

God used D. L. Moody, the nineteenth-century evangelist, to help bring two continents to repentance. He traveled more than one million miles and preached the Gospel of Jesus Christ to more than 100 million people!

What characteristics made Moody stand out as God's man to reach the masses in Europe and North America? He was a man of faith. He was a man of purity. And he was a man of prayer.

Moody said this about prayer: "Some men's prayers need to be cut short at both ends and set on fire in the middle."

Are your prayers on fire? Do your prayers reach the ear of God and move the hearts of men? Let me briefly describe the kind of prayer that God delights to answer.

We must believe that God is able and willing to answer our prayers. Hebrews 11:6 says: "Without faith it is impossible to please God, because anyone who comes to him must believe that he exists and that he rewards those who earnestly seek him." Many Christians don't believe God will grant their petitions. No wonder their prayers lack fire! The Bible teaches that God answers prayer offered in faith.

We must ask. God longs to pour out His blessings if only we will ask for them. "You do not have, because you do not ask God" (James 4:2). We beat around the bush and try to twist God's arm with our detailed petitions. Instead, we must drop the flowery words and get to the point. Eliminating the extraneous and setting our eyes on the One to whom we are talking will set our prayers aflame.

We must confess sin. The psalmist wrote, "If I had cherished sin in my heart, the Lord would not have listened" (Psalm 66:18). Unconfessed sin douses the flames of prayer.

Before each of his evangelistic campaigns, Moody urged God's people to pray. The fires of revival that swept across two nations were not lit by Moody alone. They were ignited by the prayers of ordinary Christians who believed God, confessed their sins, and then offered prayers that God delighted to answer.

THE FIVE ELEMENTS OF PRAYER

Perhaps you long to pray prayers that are on fire—prayers that God delights to answer. But you still are not sure about the specifics of prayer. How do you begin? What do you say?

Prayer is simply conversation between God and ourselves. God speaks to us through His Word and the inner witness of the Holy Spirit. We respond to God with adoration, confession, petition, intercession, and thanksgiving.

Adoration. As we enter God's presence in prayer, we begin by expressing our worship and reverence for Him. Many psalms are excellent examples of expressing adoration for God.

Confession. We cannot praise the God of holiness without developing a sense of our own impurity. The Bible teaches us that God graciously forgives us when we confess our sins (1 John 1:9).

Petitions. True prayer consists of the petitions of someone who acknowledges his or her utter need and the provisions of One who demonstrates His utter goodness. Jesus promised, "Until now you have not asked for anything in my name. Ask and you will receive, and your joy will be complete" (John 16:24).

Intercession for other people is an important spiritual responsibility that we must not neglect. The prophet Samuel told the people of Israel, "Far be it from me that I should sin against the LORD by failing to pray for you" (1 Samuel 12:23).

Thanksgiving should fill the remainder of our conversation with God. The Bible says, "Be joyful always; pray continually; give thanks in all circumstances, for this is God's will for you in Christ Jesus" (1 Thessalonians 5:16-18). We experience God's joy when we talk with Him in prayer and thank Him for His answers.

KEEPING A PRAYER NOTEBOOK

I encourage you to start a prayer notebook as a means of watching for and remembering God's answers to your prayers. My prayer notebook motivates me to pray more frequently and specifically, and it helps me sense the reality of my personal relationship with God.

When I am going through difficult circumstances, I can reflect on God's faithfulness by reviewing how He has worked in my life in the past. Without a notebook I would soon forget many of God's marvelous answers to my prayers.

On the following page you will find space to begin your own prayer notebook. Begin recording your on-fire prayers in your notebook today. Then expect God to answer in a marvelous way!

(1) Think of an area in your life where you need an answer to prayer.

(2) In your prayer notebook, write your request and the date you begin praying for that request. If there is a deadline for an answer, include that date too.

(3) Study the following Bible passages on prayer: Matthew 7:7-11; 18:19-20; Mark 10:46-52; John 16:24; Romans 8:26-27; Ephesians 6:18-20; James 5:16-18.

(4) Simply and specifically tell the Lord your request.

(5) Thank the Lord that He is going to answer your prayer (Philippians 4:6).

(6) Record the answer when it comes, and praise God for it (Colossians 4:2).

YOUR PRAYER NOTEBOOK

Date Began Praying

Date Answer Needed

God's Answer

Date God Answered Request

Date Began Praying

Date Answer Needed

God's Answer

Date God Answered Request

Date Began Praying

Date Answer Needed

God's Answer

Date God Answered Request

Date Began Praying

Date Answer Needed

God's Answer

Date God Answered Request

Life's Trials: Why Does God Allow Suffering?

Many Christians honestly struggle with the question of why God has allowed so much suffering in the world. Only by turning to the Bible can we begin to understand the problem of suffering.

Basically, there are four types of suffering. The first is that which comes as the result of natural disasters, such as an earthquake. The suffering that results from these disasters happens to both "the righteous and the unrighteous" (Matthew 5:45).

A second type of suffering can be called man's inhumanity to man. War would be classified under this type of suffering. Because of man's greed and pride, he tries to hurt his fellow man (James 4:1-2).

A third type of suffering is best seen in the life of Job in the Old Testament; it came as a result of Satan's attack on him. After receiving permission from God, Satan moved in and caused incredible suffering to Job and his family.

A fourth type of suffering is that which comes as a result of our own erroneous actions. For example, if I walk off the roof and fall to the ground, breaking my leg, I am suffering because I broke God's law of gravity. We also suffer when we break God's moral laws.

Much suffering can be traced to the evil choices we make. Some suffering is allowed by God as a punishment for sin. Often we are simply living with the consequences of our actions (Galatians 6:7-8).

Whenever people break God's laws, others are bound to suffer as well. I refer you to the story of Achan in Joshua 7. When he coveted some of the spoil from the battle of Jericho, his sin cost the lives of thirty-six men in a battle against the city of Ai. It is inevitable that others will suffer in the wake of an individual's disobedience to God.

How we respond to suffering is going to make us or break us as Christians. Circumstances often do more to *reveal* our character than to shape it. But by properly responding to trials, we can develop patience and proven character (Romans 5:3-4).

Instead of looking at our circumstances, we need to keep our eyes on Jesus Christ, the source of life. He will bring us through whatever situation we face, and as a result we will be stronger Christians, better able to serve Him because of our trials.

▼

Life's Trials:
A God Who Is Sufficient
for the Pressures of Life

Some time ago our local newspaper reported that a well-known clinical psychologist in Portland committed suicide, leaving this note to his staff:

> Tonight I feel tired, alone, and suddenly very old. The full understanding of these feelings will come only when you, too, are tired, alone, and old.

Suicides are increasing at alarming rates. Why do people surrounded by friends and family suddenly despair of life itself? Psychologists offer many solutions to that question, but only one true solution exists—Jesus Christ. Only He can meet our deepest needs when suddenly our world is falling apart.

God has plenty to say about our outer pressures, inner despair, and everyday struggles. The following verses of Scripture could be entitled "The God Who Is Sufficient for the Pressures of Life."

> Praise be to the God and Father of our Lord Jesus Christ, the Father of compassion and the God of all comfort, who com-

forts us in all our troubles, so that we can comfort those in
any trouble with the comfort we ourselves have received
from God. For just as the sufferings of Christ flow over into
our lives, so also through Christ our comfort overflows.

—2 Corinthians 1:3-5

Are you hurting inside? Do you ever feel like giving up on life?
When a crisis arises, the worst mistake you can make is to pretend
that nothing is wrong. To find relief from your problems, you must
first acknowledge them and the despair they cause. Only then can
you embrace "the Father of compassion and the God of all comfort."
It is God's nature to be merciful and compassionate. God is the
believer's source of encouragement, consolation, and forgiveness in
all circumstances.

The secret of discovering God's sufficiency is found in spending
time with Him every day. Learn to share all of your problems and
needs with Him. Say, "O Lord, I believe You are the Father of all mer-
cies and the God of all comfort. Please help me today, especially in
this situation."

You may be saying, "But, Luis, you don't understand. My situation
is different." No problem is unique. First Corinthians 10:13 says, "No
temptation has seized you except what is common to man." For God,
one situation is not more difficult than another. God has repeatedly
shown His own problem-solving ability in all kinds of human situations. "Is anything too difficult for me?" He asks us today.

Paul experienced desperate need—physically, emotionally, and
financially. Yet he declared, "And my God will meet all your needs
according to his glorious riches in Christ Jesus" (Philippians 4:19).
From personal experience Paul spoke of a God who proved sufficient
for the pressures of his life, who would stand beside him and encourage him in the midst of his severest trials. Paul knew how to flee to his
heavenly Father for comfort.

Paul so knew God's keeping power that he did far more than endure his problems—he was strengthened and blessed by them! In turn he was able to comfort others in their hardships with the same comfort he had personally received from God (see 2 Corinthians 1:6-7).

One reason we experience trials is to enable us to comfort others who are hurting. Christians who are walking with the Lord have much to share regarding the blessings God has given them in times of deep need or despair.

It's powerful when a Christian can tell someone, "Because of a similar situation I've experienced, I think I understand what you're going through. Let me share with you what God did for me."

In the ministry of comfort, God's Word comes alive and His promises become active and real. Suddenly you understand why you went through your hardship. And, praise God, it was worth it!

Paul wrote that even the most severe pressures of daily life never separate us from the tenderness and compassion of our heavenly Father. On the contrary, when we feel like our world is falling apart, God's power and grace are magnified. As a missionary once said, "Peace is not the absence of conflict. Peace is the ability to cope." The God of all comfort can provide that "copeability" in the midst of any crisis.

Paul is not saying that we won't face disappointment, suffering, or conflict in life. But he is saying that no Christian need ever despair. Why? Because we worship the God of all comfort—the God who is sufficient for every pressure of life.

Life's Trials:
Claiming God's Promises
When We Hurt

Several years ago a submarine sank, with all its crew, off the Atlantic coast of North America. When the vessel was eventually located, divers were sent down to assess the damage and the possibility of salvaging the wreck.

As the divers neared the hull of the vessel, they were surprised to hear the pounding of a message in Morse code. It was evident someone was actually alive inside the submarine. The message was a frantic question beat against the walls of the aquatic tomb: "Is there hope? Is there hope?"

You and I ponder that same question when a problem or tragedy strikes us. Who, after all, is totally free in this life from the pain of losing a loved one, the frustration of unemployment, the anguish of a fragmented home, or any of a hundred other problems?

We feel trapped by our circumstances and wonder, "Is there hope? Is there really any hope of overcoming this problem?"

Some of us reflect on Romans 8:28 in such times (emphasis mine): "We *know* that in all things God works for the good of those who love him, who have been called according to his purpose."

That promise is a solid anchor when the storms of life beat against us.

The Apostle Paul had claimed that very promise many times before he ever penned his famous letter to the Romans. As one of God's pilgrims passing through this world, he knew what it was to suffer hardship, persecution, indifference, loneliness, stonings, beatings, shipwreck, nakedness, destitution, sleeplessness, and immense pressure.

What kept Paul from going under? I believe it was his utter confidence in the God who promises to sustain us no matter what.

Are you facing a difficult problem today? Commit yourself anew to the Lord. Then take the words of Philippians 4:6-7 to heart: "Do not be anxious about anything, but in everything, by prayer and petition, with thanksgiving, present your requests to God. And the peace of God, which transcends all understanding, will guard your hearts and your minds in Christ Jesus."

When the storms of life seem overwhelming, God wants us to experience His perfect peace.

The Gospel of Luke

▼

Looking for
Some Good News?

Have you read any good news lately? Headlines from the world's newspapers and magazines reveal our utter lack of good news:

"Middle East Tensions Flare Again"
"Economic Conditions Worsen"
"Violence Increasing in Major Cities"
"World Leaders Troubled"
"War Is Imminent"

These very headlines, however, could have been written by a Middle East correspondent we know today as Dr. Luke. Almost 2,000 years ago Dr. Luke mingled among influential circles of political and religious leaders from Europe and the Middle East.

In his travels Dr. Luke met a group of men who introduced him to the most controversial leader of his day—Jesus Christ. Suddenly Luke was reporting the most important story of his life.

The Gospel of Luke as reprinted in this book is a modern translation of Luke's report of those exciting days in Palestine. The true story you are about to read is filled with racial and religious tensions, violent crimes, economic injustice, political intrigue, suspense, murder, and—surprisingly—good news!

This fast-paced story introduces you to Jesus Christ, the Man whose birth split history in two. Dr. Luke transports us back to the dramatic days of Christ's birth, His ministry among the masses, and His subsequent betrayal and murder. But that's not all!

After Jesus was crucified for crimes He never committed, He rose from the dead! Christ's death and His resurrection made it possible for us to be completely forgiven by God—forgiven for all our sins! Now we can also experience joy and peace with God and others—and eternal life. Jesus Christ is more than an ordinary man. He is God come in the flesh to be our Redeemer. When we commit our lives to Him, the good news Luke reported becomes ours to enjoy, cherish, and share with others.

Whatever your background, I challenge you to take a new look at Christ's story from the perspective of Dr. Luke—someone who walked with Christ almost 2,000 years ago. Dr. Luke knew Jesus Christ personally, just as you have come to know Him. When you finish reading the Gospel of Luke, don't be surprised to find that you know Christ on an even deeper level. Here is the good news we are all looking for.

▼

Read Through Luke in 30 Days

Day	Reading	Description
1	1:1-38	Births of John the Baptist and Jesus foretold
2	1:39-80	Mary praises God
3	2:1-52	Jesus' birth and boyhood
4	3:1-38	John the Baptist prepares the way; Jesus' baptism; Jesus' genealogy
5	4:1-30	Temptation and rejection
6	4:31-44	Healing and preaching
7	5:1-32	The first followers of Jesus
8	5:33–6:19	Jesus chooses the twelve disciples
9	6:20-49	"Love your enemies"
10	7:1-35	Who is this man?
11	7:36–8:21	Real love; true forgiveness; complete obedience
12	8:22-56	The power of Jesus

13	9:1-36	Jesus feeds the 5,000; Peter confesses Christ
14	9:37-50	True greatness
15	9:51–10:24	Working for God's kingdom
16	10:25–11:13	"Love your neighbor"
17	11:14-54	Living as God's people
18	12:1-59	Be prepared
19	13:1-35	"Enter through the narrow door"
20	14:1-35	The cost of being a disciple
21	15:1-32	Lost and found
22	16:1-31	"You cannot serve both God and Money"
23	17:1-37	Forgiveness, faith, and the coming King
24	18:1-43	Receive the kingdom of God like a little child
25	19:1-48	The King is here
26	20:1-47	Jesus' authority is questioned
27	21:1-38	"Be always on the watch"
28	22:1-71	Jesus on trial
29	23:1-56	Jesus is crucified
30	24:1-53	Jesus is alive!

▼

The Gospel of Luke
(New International Version)

DAY 1: PREPARATIONS—LUKE 1:1-38

CHAPTER 1

Introduction

1 Many have undertaken to draw up an account of the things that have been fulfilled among us, 2 just as they were handed down to us by those who from the first were eyewitnesses and servants of the word. 3 Therefore, since I myself have carefully investigated everything from the beginning, it seemed good also to me to write an orderly account for you, most excellent Theophilus, 4 so that you may know the certainty of the things you have been taught.

The Birth of John the Baptist Foretold

5 In the time of Herod king of Judea there was a priest named Zechariah, who belonged to the priestly division of Abijah; his wife Elizabeth was also a descendant of Aaron. 6 Both of them were upright in the sight of God, observing all the Lord's commandments and regulations blamelessly. 7 But they had no children, because Elizabeth was barren; and they were both well along in years.

▼

8 Once when Zechariah's division was on duty and he was serving as priest before God, 9 he was chosen by lot, according to the custom of the priesthood, to go into the temple of the Lord and burn incense. 10 And when the time for the burning of incense came, all the assembled worshipers were praying outside.

11 Then an angel of the Lord appeared to him, standing at the right side of the altar of incense. 12 When Zechariah saw him, he was startled and was gripped with fear. 13 But the angel said to him: "Do not be afraid, Zechariah; your prayer has been heard. Your wife Elizabeth will bear you a son, and you are to give him the name John. 14 He will be a joy and delight to you, and many will rejoice because of his birth, 15 for he will be great in the sight of the Lord. He is never to take wine or other fermented drink, and he will be filled with the Holy Spirit even from birth. 16 Many of the people of Israel will he bring back to the Lord their God. 17 And he will go on before the Lord, in the spirit and power of Elijah, to turn the hearts of the fathers to their children and the disobedient to the wisdom of the righteous— to make ready a people prepared for the Lord."

18 Zechariah asked the angel, "How can I be sure of this? I am an old man and my wife is well along in years."

19 The angel answered, "I am Gabriel. I stand in the presence of God, and I have been sent to speak to you and to tell you this good news. 20 And now you will be silent and not able to speak until the day this happens, because you did not believe my words, which will come true at their proper time."

21 Meanwhile, the people were waiting for Zechariah and wondering why he stayed so long in the temple. 22 When he came out, he could not speak to them. They realized he had seen a vision in the temple, for he kept making signs to them but remained unable to speak.

23 When his time of service was completed, he returned home. 24 After this his wife Elizabeth became pregnant and for five months remained in seclusion. 25 "The Lord has done this for me," she said.

"In these days he has shown his favor and taken away my disgrace among the people."

The Birth of Jesus Foretold

26 In the sixth month, God sent the angel Gabriel to Nazareth, a town in Galilee, 27 to a virgin pledged to be married to a man named Joseph, a descendant of David. The virgin's name was Mary. 28 The angel went to her and said, "Greetings, you who are highly favored! The Lord is with you."

29 Mary was greatly troubled at his words and wondered what kind of greeting this might be. 30 But the angel said to her, "Do not be afraid, Mary, you have found favor with God. 31 You will be with child and give birth to a son, and you are to give him the name Jesus. 32 He will be great and will be called the Son of the Most High. The Lord God will give him the throne of his father David, 33 and he will reign over the house of Jacob forever; his kingdom will never end."

34 "How will this be," Mary asked the angel, "since I am a virgin?"

35 The angel answered, "The Holy Spirit will come upon you, and the power of the Most High will overshadow you. So the holy one to be born will be called the Son of God. 36 Even Elizabeth your relative is going to have a child in her old age, and she who was said to be barren is in her sixth month. 37 For nothing is impossible with God."

38 "I am the Lord's servant," Mary answered. "May it be to me as you have said." Then the angel left her.

DAY 2: GROWING EXCITEMENT—LUKE 1:39-80

Mary Visits Elizabeth

39 At that time Mary got ready and hurried to a town in the hill country of Judea, 40 where she entered Zechariah's home and greeted Elizabeth.

41 When Elizabeth heard Mary's greeting, the baby leaped in her womb, and Elizabeth was filled with the Holy Spirit. 42 In a loud voice

she exclaimed: "Blessed are you among women, and blessed is the child you will bear! 43 But why am I so favored, that the mother of my Lord should come to me? 44 As soon as the sound of your greeting reached my ears, the baby in my womb leaped for joy. 45 Blessed is she who has believed that what the Lord has said to her will be accomplished!"

Mary's Song

46 And Mary said: "My soul praises the Lord 47 and my spirit rejoices in God my Savior, 48 for he has been mindful of the humble state of his servant. From now on all generations will call me blessed, 49 for the Mighty One has done great things for me—holy is his name. 50 His mercy extends to those who fear him, from generation to generation. 51 He has performed mighty deeds with his arm; he has scattered those who are proud in their inmost thoughts. 52 He has brought down rulers from their thrones but has lifted up the humble. 53 He has filled the hungry with good things but has sent the rich away empty. 54 He has helped his servant Israel, remembering to be merciful 55 to Abraham and his descendants forever, even as he said to our fathers."

56 Mary stayed with Elizabeth for about three months and then returned home.

The Birth of John the Baptist

57 When it was time for Elizabeth to have her baby, she gave birth to a son. 58 Her neighbors and relatives heard that the Lord had shown her great mercy, and they shared her joy.

59 On the eighth day they came to circumcise the child, and they were going to name him after his father Zechariah, 60 but his mother spoke up and said, "No! He is to be called John."

61 They said to her, "There is no one among your relatives who has that name."

62 Then they made signs to his father, to find out what he would like to name the child. 63 He asked for a writing tablet, and to every-

one's astonishment he wrote, "His name is John." 64 Immediately his mouth was opened and his tongue was loosed, and he began to speak, praising God. 65 The neighbors were all filled with awe, and throughout the hill country of Judea people were talking about all these things. 66 Everyone who heard this wondered about it, asking, "What then is this child going to be?" For the Lord's hand was with him.

Zechariah's Song

67 His father Zechariah was filled with the Holy Spirit and prophesied: 68 "Praise be to the Lord, the God of Israel, because he has come and has redeemed his people. 69 He has raised up a horn of salvation for us in the house of his servant David 70 (as he said through his holy prophets of long ago), 71 salvation from our enemies and from the hand of all who hate us— 72 to show mercy to our fathers and to remember his holy covenant, 73 the oath he swore to our father Abraham: 74 to rescue us from the hand of our enemies, and to enable us to serve him without fear 75 in holiness and righteousness before him all our days. 76 And you, my child, will be called a prophet of the Most High; for you will go on before the Lord to prepare the way for him, 77 to give his people the knowledge of salvation through the forgiveness of their sins, 78 because of the tender mercy of our God, by which the rising sun will come to us from heaven 79 to shine on those living in darkness and in the shadow of death, to guide our feet into the path of peace."

80 And the child grew and became strong in spirit; and he lived in the desert until he appeared publicly to Israel.

DAY 3: JESUS' EARLY YEARS—LUKE 2:1-52

CHAPTER 2

The Birth of Jesus

1 In those days Caesar Augustus issued a decree that a census should be taken of the entire Roman world. 2 (This was the first cen-

sus that took place while Quirinius was governor of Syria.) 3 And everyone went to his own town to register.

4 So Joseph also went up from the town of Nazareth in Galilee to Judea, to Bethlehem the town of David, because he belonged to the house and line of David. 5 He went there to register with Mary, who was pledged to be married to him and was expecting a child. 6 While they were there, the time came for the baby to be born, 7 and she gave birth to her firstborn, a son. She wrapped him in cloths and placed him in a manger, because there was no room for them in the inn.

The Shepherds and the Angels

8 And there were shepherds living out in the fields nearby, keeping watch over their flocks at night. 9 An angel of the Lord appeared to them, and the glory of the Lord shone around them, and they were terrified. 10 But the angel said to them, "Do not be afraid. I bring you good news of great joy that will be for all the people. 11 Today in the town of David a Savior has been born to you; he is Christ the Lord. 12This will be a sign to you: You will find a baby wrapped in cloths and lying in a manger."

13 Suddenly a great company of the heavenly host appeared with the angel, praising God and saying, 14 "Glory to God in the highest, and on earth peace to men on whom his favor rests."

15When the angels had left them and gone into heaven, the shepherds said to one another, "Let's go to Bethlehem and see this thing that has happened, which the Lord has told us about."

16 So they hurried off and found Mary and Joseph, and the baby, who was lying in the manger. 17 When they had seen him, they spread the word concerning what had been told them about this child, 18 and all who heard it were amazed at what the shepherds said to them. 19 But Mary treasured up all these things and pondered them in her heart. 20The shepherds returned, glorifying and praising God for all the things they had heard and seen, which were just as they had been told.

Jesus Presented in the Temple

21 On the eighth day, when it was time to circumcise him, he was named Jesus, the name the angel had given him before he had been conceived.

22 When the time of their purification according to the Law of Moses had been completed, Joseph and Mary took him to Jerusalem to present him to the Lord 23 (as it is written in the Law of the Lord, "Every firstborn male is to be consecrated to the Lord"), 24 and to offer a sacrifice in keeping with what is said in the Law of the Lord: "a pair of doves or two young pigeons."

25 Now there was a man in Jerusalem called Simeon, who was righteous and devout. He was waiting for the consolation of Israel, and the Holy Spirit was upon him. 26 It had been revealed to him by the Holy Spirit that he would not die before he had seen the Lord's Christ. 27 Moved by the Spirit, he went into the temple courts. When the parents brought in the child Jesus to do for him what the custom of the Law required, 28 Simeon took him in his arms and praised God, saying: 29 "Sovereign Lord, as you have promised, you now dismiss your servant in peace. 30 For my eyes have seen your salvation, 31 which you have prepared in the sight of all people, 32 a light for revelation to the Gentiles and for glory to your people Israel."

33 The child's father and mother marveled at what was said about him. 34 Then Simeon blessed them and said to Mary, his mother: "This child is destined to cause the falling and rising of many in Israel, and to be a sign that will be spoken against, 35 so that the thoughts of many hearts will be revealed. And a sword will pierce your own soul too."

36 There was also a prophetess, Anna, the daughter of Phanuel, of the tribe of Asher. She was very old; she had lived with her husband seven years after her marriage, 37 and then was a widow until she was eighty-four. She never left the temple but worshiped night and day, fasting and praying. 38 Coming up to them at that very moment, she

gave thanks to God and spoke about the child to all who were looking forward to the redemption of Jerusalem.

39 When Joseph and Mary had done everything required by the Law of the Lord, they returned to Galilee to their own town of Nazareth. 40 And the child grew and became strong; he was filled with wisdom, and the grace of God was upon him.

The Boy Jesus at the Temple

41 Every year his parents went to Jerusalem for the Feast of the Passover. 42 When he was twelve years old, they went up to the Feast, according to the custom. 43 After the Feast was over, while his parents were returning home, the boy Jesus stayed behind in Jerusalem, but they were unaware of it. 44 Thinking he was in their company, they traveled on for a day. Then they began looking for him among their relatives and friends. 45 When they did not find him, they went back to Jerusalem to look for him. 46 After three days they found him in the temple courts, sitting among the teachers, listening to them and asking them questions. 47 Everyone who heard him was amazed at his understanding and his answers. 48 When his parents saw him, they were astonished. His mother said to him, "Son, why have you treated us like this? Your father and I have been anxiously searching for you."

49 "Why were you searching for me?" he asked. "Didn't you know I had to be in my Father's house?" 50 But they did not understand what he was saying to them.

51 Then he went down to Nazareth with them and was obedient to them. But his mother treasured all these things in her heart. 52 And Jesus grew in wisdom and stature, and in favor with God and men.

DAY 4: GETTING READY —LUKE 3:1-38

CHAPTER 3

John the Baptist Prepares the Way

1 In the fifteenth year of the reign of Tiberius Caesar—when

Pontius Pilate was governor of Judea, Herod tetrarch of Galilee, his brother Philip tetrarch of Iturea and Traconitis, and Lysanias tetrarch of Abilene— 2 during the high priesthood of Annas and Caiaphas, the word of God came to John son of Zechariah in the desert. 3 He went into all the country around the Jordan, preaching a baptism of repentance for the forgiveness of sins. 4 As is written in the book of the words of Isaiah the prophet: "A voice of one calling in the desert, 'Prepare the way for the Lord, make straight paths for him. 5 Every valley shall be filled in, every mountain and hill made low. The crooked roads shall become straight, the rough ways smooth. 6 And all mankind will see God's salvation.'"

7 John said to the crowds coming out to be baptized by him, "You brood of vipers! Who warned you to flee from the coming wrath? 8Produce fruit in keeping with repentance. And do not begin to say to yourselves, 'We have Abraham as our father.' For I tell you that out of these stones God can raise up children for Abraham. 9 The ax is already at the root of the trees, and every tree that does not produce good fruit will be cut down and thrown into the fire."

10 "What should we do then?" the crowd asked.

11 John answered, "The man with two tunics should share with him who has none, and the one who has food should do the same."

12 Tax collectors also came to be baptized. "Teacher," they asked, "what should we do?"

13 "Don't collect any more than you are required to," he told them.

14 Then some soldiers asked him, "And what should we do?"

He replied, "Don't extort money and don't accuse people falsely— be content with your pay."

15 The people were waiting expectantly and were all wondering in their hearts if John might possibly be the Christ. 16 John answered them all, "I baptize you with water. But one more powerful than I will come, the thongs of whose sandals I am not worthy to untie. He will baptize you with the Holy Spirit and with fire. 17 His winnowing fork

is in his hand to clear his threshing floor and to gather the wheat into his barn, but he will burn up the chaff with unquenchable fire." [18] And with many other words John exhorted the people and preached the good news to them.

[19] But when John rebuked Herod the tetrarch because of Herodias, his brother's wife, and all the other evil things he had done, [20] Herod added this to them all: He locked John up in prison.

The Baptism and Genealogy of Jesus

[21] When all the people were being baptized, Jesus was baptized too. And as he was praying, heaven was opened [22] and the Holy Spirit descended on him in bodily form like a dove. And a voice came from heaven: "You are my Son, whom I love; with you I am well pleased."

[23] Now Jesus himself was about thirty years old when he began his ministry. He was the son, so it was thought, of Joseph, the son of Heli,[24] the son of Matthat, the son of Levi, the son of Melki, the son of Jannai, the son of Joseph, [25] the son of Mattathias, the son of Amos, the son of Nahum, the son of Esli, the son of Naggai, [26] the son of Maath, the son of Mattathias, the son of Semein, the son of Josech, the son of Joda, [27] the son of Joanan, the son of Rhesa, the son of Zerubbabel, the son of Shealtiel, the son of Neri, [28] the son of Melki, the son of Addi, the son of Cosam, the son of Elmadam, the son of Er, [29] the son of Joshua, the son of Eliezer, the son of Jorim, the son of Matthat, the son of Levi, [30] the son of Simeon, the son of Judah, the son of Joseph, the son of Jonam, the son of Eliakim, [31] the son of Melea, the son of Menna, the son of Mattatha, the son of Nathan, the son of David, [32] the son of Jesse, the son of Obed, the son of Boaz, the son of Salmon, the son of Nahshon, [33] the son of Amminadab, the son of Ram, the son of Hezron, the son of Perez, the son of Judah, [34] the son of Jacob, the son of Isaac, the son of Abraham, the son of Terah, the son of Nahor, [35] the son of Serug, the son of Reu, the son of Peleg, the son of Eber, the son of Shelah, [36] the son of Cainan, the son of

Arphaxad, the son of Shem, the son of Noah, the son of Lamech, 37 the son of Methuselah, the son of Enoch, the son of Jared, the son of Mahalalel, the son of Cainan, 38 the son of Enos, the son of Seth, the son of Adam, the son of God.

DAY 5: TEMPTATION AND REJECTION—LUKE 4:1-30

CHAPTER 4

The Temptation of Jesus

1 Jesus, full of the Holy Spirit, returned from the Jordan and was led by the Spirit in the desert, 2 where for forty days he was tempted by the devil. He ate nothing during those days, and at the end of them he was hungry.

3 The devil said to him, "If you are the Son of God, tell this stone to become bread."

4 Jesus answered, "It is written: 'Man does not live on bread alone.'"

5 The devil led him up to a high place and showed him in an instant all the kingdoms of the world. 6 And he said to him, "I will give you all their authority and splendor, for it has been given to me, and I can give it to anyone I want to. 7 So if you worship me, it will all be yours."

8 Jesus answered, "It is written: 'Worship the Lord your God and serve him only.'"

9 The devil led him to Jerusalem and had him stand on the highest point of the temple. "If you are the Son of God," he said, "throw yourself down from here. 10 For it is written: 'He will command his angels concerning you to guard you carefully; 11 they will lift you up in their hands, so that you will not strike your foot against a stone.'"

12 Jesus answered, "It says: 'Do not put the Lord your God to the test.'"

13 When the devil had finished all this tempting, he left him until an opportune time.

▼

Jesus Rejected at Nazareth

[14] Jesus returned to Galilee in the power of the Spirit, and news about him spread through the whole countryside. [15] He taught in their synagogues, and everyone praised him.

[16] He went to Nazareth, where he had been brought up, and on the Sabbath day he went into the synagogue, as was his custom. And he stood up to read. [17] The scroll of the prophet Isaiah was handed to him. Unrolling it, he found the place where it is written: [18] "The Spirit of the Lord is on me, because he has anointed me to preach good news to the poor. He has sent me to proclaim freedom for the prisoners and recovery of sight for the blind, to release the oppressed, [19] to proclaim the year of the Lord's favor."

[20] Then he rolled up the scroll, gave it back to the attendant and sat down. The eyes of everyone in the synagogue were fastened on him, [21] and he began by saying to them, "Today this scripture is fulfilled in your hearing."

[22] All spoke well of him and were amazed at the gracious words that came from his lips. "Isn't this Joseph's son?" they asked.

[23] Jesus said to them, "Surely you will quote this proverb to me: 'Physician, heal yourself! Do here in your home town what we have heard that you did in Capernaum.'

[24] "I tell you the truth," he continued, "no prophet is accepted in his home town. [25] I assure you that there were many widows in Israel in Elijah's time, when the sky was shut for three and a half years and there was a severe famine throughout the land. [26] Yet Elijah was not sent to any of them, but to a widow in Zarephath in the region of Sidon. [27] And there were many in Israel with leprosy in the time of Elisha the prophet, yet not one of them was cleansed—only Naaman the Syrian."

[28] All the people in the synagogue were furious when they heard this. [29] They got up, drove him out of the town, and took him to the brow of the hill on which the town was built, in order to throw him

down the cliff. 30 But he walked right through the crowd and went on his way.

DAY 6: HEALING AND PREACHING—LUKE 4:31-44

Jesus Drives Out an Evil Spirit

31 Then he went down to Capernaum, a town in Galilee, and on the Sabbath began to teach the people. 32 They were amazed at his teaching, because his message had authority.

33 In the synagogue there was a man possessed by a demon, an evil spirit. He cried out at the top of his voice, 34 "Ha! What do you want with us, Jesus of Nazareth? Have you come to destroy us? I know who you are—the Holy One of God!"

35 "Be quiet!" Jesus said sternly. "Come out of him!" Then the demon threw the man down before them all and came out without injuring him.

36 All the people were amazed and said to each other, "What is this teaching? With authority and power he gives orders to evil spirits and they come out!" 37 And the news about him spread throughout the surrounding area.

Jesus Heals Many

38 Jesus left the synagogue and went to the home of Simon. Now Simon's mother-in-law was suffering from a high fever, and they asked Jesus to help her. 39 So he bent over her and rebuked the fever, and it left her. She got up at once and began to wait on them.

40 When the sun was setting, the people brought to Jesus all who had various kinds of sickness, and laying his hands on each one, he healed them. 41 Moreover, demons came out of many people, shouting, "You are the Son of God!" But he rebuked them and would not allow them to speak, because they knew he was the Christ.

42 At daybreak Jesus went out to a solitary place. The people were looking for him and when they came to where he was, they tried to keep

him from leaving them. [43] But he said, "I must preach the good news of the kingdom of God to the other towns also, because that is why I was sent." [44] And he kept on preaching in the synagogues of Judea.

DAY 7: THE FIRST FOLLOWERS OF JESUS—LUKE 5:1-32

CHAPTER 5

The Calling of the First Disciples

[1] One day as Jesus was standing by the Lake of Gennesaret, with the people crowding around him and listening to the word of God, [2] he saw at the water's edge two boats, left there by the fishermen, who were washing their nets. [3] He got into one of the boats, the one belonging to Simon, and asked him to put out a little from shore. Then he sat down and taught the people from the boat.

[4] When he had finished speaking, he said to Simon, "Put out into deep water, and let down the nets for a catch."

[5] Simon answered, "Master, we've worked hard all night and haven't caught anything. But because you say so, I will let down the nets."

[6] When they had done so, they caught such a large number of fish that their nets began to break. [7] So they signaled their partners in the other boat to come and help them, and they came and filled both boats so full that they began to sink.

[8] When Simon Peter saw this, he fell at Jesus' knees and said, "Go away from me, Lord; I am a sinful man!" [9] For he and all his companions were astonished at the catch of fish they had taken, [10] and so were James and John, the sons of Zebedee, Simon's partners.

Then Jesus said to Simon, "Don't be afraid; from now on you will catch men." [11] So they pulled their boats up on shore, left everything and followed him.

The Man with Leprosy

[12] While Jesus was in one of the towns, a man came along who was covered with leprosy. When he saw Jesus, he fell with his face to

the ground and begged him, "Lord, if you are willing, you can make me clean."

13 Jesus reached out his hand and touched the man. "I am willing," he said. "Be clean!" And immediately the leprosy left him.

14 Then Jesus ordered him, "Don't tell anyone, but go, show yourself to the priest and offer the sacrifices that Moses commanded for your cleansing, as a testimony to them."

15 Yet the news about him spread all the more, so that crowds of people came to hear him and to be healed of their sicknesses. 16 But Jesus often withdrew to lonely places and prayed.

Jesus Heals a Paralytic

17 One day as he was teaching, Pharisees and teachers of the law, who had come from every village of Galilee and from Judea and Jerusalem, were sitting there. And the power of the Lord was present for him to heal the sick. 18 Some men came carrying a paralytic on a mat and tried to take him into the house to lay him before Jesus. 19When they could not find a way to do this because of the crowd, they went up on the roof and lowered him on his mat through the tiles into the middle of the crowd, right in front of Jesus.

20 When Jesus saw their faith, he said, "Friend, your sins are forgiven."

21 The Pharisees and the teachers of the law began thinking to themselves, "Who is this fellow who speaks blasphemy? Who can forgive sins but God alone?"

22 Jesus knew what they were thinking and asked, "Why are you thinking these things in your hearts? 23 Which is easier: to say, 'Your sins are forgiven,' or to say, 'Get up and walk'? 24 But that you may know that the Son of Man has authority on earth to forgive sins . . ." He said to the paralyzed man, "I tell you, get up, take your mat and go home." 25 Immediately he stood up in front of them, took what he had been lying on and went home praising God. 26 Everyone was amazed

▼

and gave praise to God. They were filled with awe and said, "We have seen remarkable things today."

The Calling of Levi

27 After this, Jesus went out and saw a tax collector by the name of Levi sitting at his tax booth. "Follow me," Jesus said to him, 28 and Levi got up, left everything and followed him.

29 Then Levi held a great banquet for Jesus at his house, and a large crowd of tax collectors and others were eating with them. 30 But the Pharisees and the teachers of the law who belonged to their sect complained to his disciples, "Why do you eat and drink with tax collectors and sinners?"

31 Jesus answered them, "It is not the healthy who need a doctor, but the sick. 32 I have not come to call the righteous, but sinners to repentance."

DAY 8: DIFFICULT QUESTIONS—LUKE 5:33–6:19

Jesus Questioned About Fasting

33 They said to him, "John's disciples often fast and pray, and so do the disciples of the Pharisees, but yours go on eating and drinking."

34 Jesus answered, "Can you make the guests of the bridegroom fast while he is with them? 35 But the time will come when the bridegroom will be taken from them; in those days they will fast."

36 He told them this parable: "No one tears a patch from a new garment and sews it on an old one. If he does, he will have torn the new garment, and the patch from the new will not match the old. 37And no one pours new wine into old wineskins. If he does, the new wine will burst the skins, the wine will run out and the wineskins will be ruined. 38 No, new wine must be poured into new wineskins. 39 And no one, after drinking old wine wants the new, for he says, 'The old is better.'"

CHAPTER 6

Lord of the Sabbath

1 One Sabbath Jesus was going through the grainfields, and his disciples began to pick some heads of grain, rub them in their hands and eat the kernels. 2 Some of the Pharisees asked, "Why are you doing what is unlawful on the Sabbath?"

3 Jesus answered them, "Have you never read what David did when he and his companions were hungry? 4 He entered the house of God, and taking the consecrated bread, he ate what is lawful only for priests to eat. And he also gave some to his companions." 5 Then Jesus said to them, "The Son of Man is Lord of the Sabbath."

6 On another Sabbath he went into the synagogue and was teaching, and a man was there whose right hand was shriveled. 7 The Pharisees and the teachers of the law were looking for a reason to accuse Jesus, so they watched him closely to see if he would heal on the Sabbath. 8 But Jesus knew what they were thinking and said to the man with the shriveled hand, "Get up and stand in front of everyone." So he got up and stood there.

9 Then Jesus said to them, "I ask you, which is lawful on the Sabbath: to do good or to do evil, to save life or to destroy it?"

10 He looked around at them all, and then said to the man, "Stretch out your hand." He did so, and his hand was completely restored. 11 But they were furious and began to discuss with one another what they might do to Jesus.

The Twelve Apostles

12 One of those days Jesus went out into the hills to pray, and spent the night praying to God. 13 When morning came, he called his disciples to him and chose twelve of them, whom he also designated apostles: 14 Simon (whom he named Peter), his brother Andrew, James, John, Philip, Bartholomew, 15 Matthew, Thomas, James son of

Alphaeus, Simon who was called the Zealot, [16] Judas son of James, and Judas Iscariot, who became a traitor.

Blessings and Woes

[17] He went down with them and stood on a level place. A large crowd of his disciples was there and a great number of people from all over Judea, from Jerusalem, and from the seacoast of Tyre and Sidon, [18] who had come to hear him and to be healed of their diseases. Those troubled by evil spirits were cured, [19] and the people all tried to touch him, because power was coming from him and healing them all.

DAY 9: "LOVE YOUR ENEMIES"—LUKE 6:20-49

[20] Looking at his disciples, he said: "Blessed are you who are poor, for yours is the kingdom of God. [21] Blessed are you who hunger now, for you will be satisfied. Blessed are you who weep now, for you will laugh. [22] Blessed are you when men hate you, when they exclude you and insult you and reject your name as evil, because of the Son of Man. [23] Rejoice in that day and leap for joy, because great is your reward in heaven. For that is how their fathers treated the prophets. [24] But woe to you who are rich, for you have already received your comfort. [25] Woe to you who are well fed now, for you will go hungry. Woe to you who laugh now, for you will mourn and weep. [26] Woe to you when all men speak well of you, for that is how their fathers treated the false prophets."

Love for Enemies

[27] "But I tell you who hear me: Love your enemies, do good to those who hate you, [28] bless those who curse you, pray for those who mistreat you. [29] If someone strikes you on one cheek, turn to him the other also. If someone takes your cloak, do not stop him from taking your tunic. [30] Give to everyone who asks you, and if anyone takes what belongs to you, do not demand it back. [31] Do to others as you would have them do to you.

32 "If you love those who love you, what credit is that to you? Even 'sinners' love those who love them. 33 And if you do good to those who are good to you, what credit is that to you? Even 'sinners' do that. 34 And if you lend to those from whom you expect repayment, what credit is that to you? Even 'sinners' lend to 'sinners,' expecting to be repaid in full. 35 But love your enemies, do good to them, and lend to them without expecting to get anything back. Then your reward will be great, and you will be sons of the Most High, because he is kind to the ungrateful and wicked. 36 Be merciful, just as your Father is merciful."

Judging Others

37 "Do not judge, and you will not be judged. Do not condemn, and you will not be condemned. Forgive, and you will be forgiven. 38 Give, and it will be given to you. A good measure, pressed down, shaken together and running over, will be poured into your lap. For with the measure you use, it will be measured to you."

39 He also told them this parable: "Can a blind man lead a blind man? Will they not both fall into a pit? 40 A student is not above his teacher, but everyone who is fully trained will be like his teacher.

41 "Why do you look at the speck of sawdust in your brother's eye and pay no attention to the plank in your own eye? 42 How can you say to your brother, 'Brother, let me take the speck out of your eye,' when you yourself fail to see the plank in your own eye? You hypocrite, first take the plank out of your eye, and then you will see clearly to remove the speck from your brother's eye."

A Tree and Its Fruit

43 "No good tree bears bad fruit, nor does a bad tree bear good fruit. 44 Each tree is recognized by its own fruit. People do not pick figs from thornbushes, or grapes from briers. 45 The good man brings good things out of the good stored up in his heart, and the evil man brings evil things out of the evil stored up in his heart. For out of the overflow of his heart his mouth speaks."

The Wise and Foolish Builders

46 "Why do you call me, 'Lord, Lord,' and do not do what I say? 47 I will show you what he is like who comes to me and hears my words and puts them into practice. 48 He is like a man building a house, who dug down deep and laid the foundation on rock. When a flood came, the torrent struck that house but could not shake it, because it was well built. 49 But the one who hears my words and does not put them into practice is like a man who built a house on the ground without a foundation. The moment the torrent struck that house, it collapsed and its destruction was complete."

<u>DAY 10: WHO IS THIS MAN?—LUKE 7:1-35</u>

CHAPTER 7

The Faith of the Centurion

1 When Jesus had finished saying all this in the hearing of the people, he entered Capernaum. 2 There a centurion's servant, whom his master valued highly, was sick and about to die. 3 The centurion heard of Jesus and sent some elders of the Jews to him, asking him to come and heal his servant. 4 When they came to Jesus, they pleaded earnestly with him, "This man deserves to have you do this, 5 because he loves our nation and has built our synagogue." 6 So Jesus went with them.

He was not far from the house when the centurion sent friends to say to him: "Lord, don't trouble yourself, for I do not deserve to have you come under my roof. 7 That is why I did not even consider myself worthy to come to you. But say the word, and my servant will be healed. 8 For I myself am a man under authority, with soldiers under me. I tell this one, 'Go,' and he goes; and that one, 'Come,' and he comes. I say to my servant, 'Do this,' and he does it."

9 When Jesus heard this, he was amazed at him, and turning to the crowd following him, he said, "I tell you, I have not found such

great faith even in Israel." [10] Then the men who had been sent returned to the house and found the servant well.

Jesus Raises a Widow's Son

[11] Soon afterward, Jesus went to a town called Nain, and his disciples and a large crowd went along with him. [12] As he approached the town gate, a dead person was being carried out—the only son of his mother, and she was a widow. And a large crowd from the town was with her. [13] When the Lord saw her, his heart went out to her and he said, "Don't cry."

[14] Then he went up and touched the coffin, and those carrying it stood still. He said, "Young man, I say to you, get up!" [15] The dead man sat up and began to talk, and Jesus gave him back to his mother.

[16] They were all filled with awe and praised God. "A great prophet has appeared among us," they said. "God has come to help his people." [17] This news about Jesus spread throughout Judea and the surrounding country.

Jesus and John the Baptist

[18] John's disciples told him about all these things. Calling two of them, [19] he sent them to the Lord to ask, "Are you the one who was to come, or should we expect someone else?"

[20] When the men came to Jesus, they said, "John the Baptist sent us to you to ask, 'Are you the one who was to come, or should we expect someone else?'"

[21] At that very time Jesus cured many who had diseases, sicknesses and evil spirits, and gave sight to many who were blind. [22] So he replied to the messengers, "Go back and report to John what you have seen and heard: The blind receive sight, the lame walk, those who have leprosy are cured, the deaf hear, the dead are raised, and the good news is preached to the poor. [23] Blessed is the man who does not fall away on account of me."

[24] After John's messengers left, Jesus began to speak to the crowd

▼

about John: "What did you go out into the desert to see? A reed swayed by the wind? 25 If not, what did you go out to see? A man dressed in fine clothes? No, those who wear expensive clothes and indulge in luxury are in palaces. 26 But what did you go out to see? A prophet? Yes, I tell you, and more than a prophet. 27 This is the one about whom it is written: 'I will send my messenger ahead of you, who will prepare your way before you.' 28 I tell you, among those born of women there is no one greater than John; yet the one who is least in the kingdom of God is greater than he."

29 (All the people, even the tax collectors, when they heard Jesus' words, acknowledged that God's way was right, because they had been baptized by John. 30 But the Pharisees and experts in the law rejected God's purpose for themselves, because they had not been baptized by John.)

31 "To what, then, can I compare the people of this generation? What are they like? 32 They are like children sitting in the market-place and calling out to each other: 'We played the flute for you, and you did not dance; we sang a dirge, and you did not cry.' 33 For John the Baptist came neither eating bread nor drinking wine, and you say, 'He has a demon.' 34 The Son of Man came eating and drinking, and you say, 'Here is a glutton and a drunkard, a friend of tax collectors and "sinners."' 35 But wisdom is proved right by all her children."

DAY 11: REAL LOVE; TRUE FORGIVENESS; COMPLETE OBEDIENCE—LUKE 7:36–8:21

Jesus Anointed by a Sinful Woman

36 Now one of the Pharisees invited Jesus to have dinner with him, so he went to the Pharisee's house and reclined at the table. 37 When a woman who had lived a sinful life in that town learned that Jesus was eating at the Pharisee's house, she brought an alabaster jar of per-

fume, [38] and as she stood behind him at his feet weeping, she began to wet his feet with her tears. Then she wiped them with her hair, kissed them and poured perfume on them. [39] When the Pharisee who had invited him saw this, he said to himself, "If this man were a prophet, he would know who is touching him and what kind of woman she is—that she is a sinner."

[40] Jesus answered him, "Simon, I have something to tell you."

"Tell me, teacher," he said.

[41] "Two men owed money to a certain moneylender. One owed him five hundred denarii, and the other fifty. [42] Neither of them had the money to pay him back, so he canceled the debts of both. Now which of them will love him more?"

[43] Simon replied, "I suppose the one who had the bigger debt canceled."

"You have judged correctly," Jesus said.

[44] Then he turned toward the woman and said to Simon, "Do you see this woman? I came into your house. You did not give me any water for my feet, but she wet my feet with her tears and wiped them with her hair. [45] You did not give me a kiss, but this woman, from the time I entered, has not stopped kissing my feet. [46] You did not put oil on my head, but she has poured perfume on my feet. [47] Therefore, I tell you, her many sins have been forgiven—for she loved much. But he who has been forgiven little loves little."

[48] Then Jesus said to her, "Your sins are forgiven."

[49] The other guests began to say among themselves, "Who is this who even forgives sins?"

[50] Jesus said to the woman, "Your faith has saved you; go in peace."

CHAPTER 8

The Parable of the Sower

[1] After this, Jesus traveled about from one town and village to

▼

another, proclaiming the good news of the kingdom of God. The Twelve were with him, 2 and also some women who had been cured of evil spirits and diseases: Mary (called Magdalene) from whom seven demons had come out; 3 Joanna the wife of Cuza, the manager of Herod's household; Susanna; and many others. These women were helping to support them out of their own means.

4 While a large crowd was gathering and people were coming to Jesus from town after town, he told this parable: 5 "A farmer went out to sow his seed. As he was scattering the seed, some fell along the path; it was trampled on, and the birds of the air ate it up. 6 Some fell on rock, and when it came up, the plants withered because they had no moisture. 7 Other seed fell among thorns, which grew up with it and choked the plants. 8 Still other seed fell on good soil. It came up and yielded a crop, a hundred times more than was sown."

When he said this, he called out, "He who has ears to hear, let him hear."

9 His disciples asked him what this parable meant. 10 He said, "The knowledge of the secrets of the kingdom of God has been given to you, but to others I speak in parables, so that, 'though seeing, they cannot see; though hearing, they may not understand.'

11 "This is the meaning of the parable: The seed is the word of God. 12 Those along the path are the ones who hear, and then the devil comes and takes away the word from their hearts, so that they cannot believe and be saved. 13 Those on the rock are the ones who receive the word with joy when they hear it, but they have no root. They believe for a while, but in the time of testing they fall away. 14 The seed that fell among thorns stands for those who hear, but as they go on their way they are choked by life's worries, riches and pleasures, and they do not mature. 15 But the seed on good soil stands for those with a noble and good heart, who hear the word, retain it, and by persevering produce a crop."

A Lamp on a Stand

16 "No one lights a lamp and hides it in a jar or puts it under a bed. Instead, he puts it on a stand, so that those who come in can see the light. 17 For there is nothing hidden that will not be disclosed, and nothing concealed that will not be known or brought out into the open. 18 Therefore consider carefully how you listen. Whoever has will be given more; whoever does not have, even what he thinks he has will be taken from him."

Jesus' Mother and Brothers

19 Now Jesus' mother and brothers came to see him, but they were not able to get near him because of the crowd. 20 Someone told him, "Your mother and brothers are standing outside, wanting to see you."

21 He replied, "My mother and brothers are those who hear God's word and put it into practice."

DAY 12: THE POWER OF JESUS—LUKE 8:22-56

Jesus Calms the Storm

22 One day Jesus said to his disciples, "Let's go over to the other side of the lake." So they got into a boat and set out. 23 As they sailed, he fell asleep. A squall came down on the lake, so that the boat was being swamped, and they were in great danger.

24 The disciples went and woke him, saying, "Master, Master, we're going to drown!"

He got up and rebuked the wind and the raging waters; the storm subsided, and all was calm. 25 "Where is your faith?" he asked his disciples.

In fear and amazement they asked one another, "Who is this? He commands even the winds and the water, and they obey him."

The Healing of a Demon-possessed Man

26 They sailed to the region of the Gerasenes, which is across the

lake from Galilee. 27 When Jesus stepped ashore, he was met by a
demon-possessed man from the town. For a long time this man had
not worn clothes or lived in a house, but had lived in the tombs.
28When he saw Jesus, he cried out and fell at his feet, shouting at the
top of his voice, "What do you want with me, Jesus, Son of the Most
High God? I beg you, don't torture me!" 29 For Jesus had commanded
the evil spirit to come out of the man. Many times it had seized him,
and though he was chained hand and foot and kept under guard, he
had broken his chains and had been driven by the demon into solitary places.

30 Jesus asked him, "What is your name?"

"Legion," he replied, because many demons had gone into him.
31 And they begged him repeatedly not to order them to go into the
Abyss.

32 A large herd of pigs was feeding there on the hillside. The
demons begged Jesus to let them go into them, and he gave them permission. 33 When the demons came out of the man, they went into the
pigs, and the herd rushed down the steep bank into the lake and was
drowned.

34 When those tending the pigs saw what had happened, they ran
off and reported this in the town and countryside, 35 and the people
went out to see what had happened. When they came to Jesus, they
found the man from whom the demons had gone out, sitting at Jesus'
feet, dressed and in his right mind; and they were afraid. 36 Those who
had seen it told the people how the demon-possessed man had been
cured. 37 Then all the people of the region of the Gerasenes asked
Jesus to leave them, because they were overcome with fear. So he got
into the boat and left.

38 The man from whom the demons had gone out begged to go
with him, but Jesus sent him away, saying, 39 "Return home and tell
how much God has done for you." So the man went away and told all
over town how much Jesus had done for him.

A Dead Girl and a Sick Woman

40 Now when Jesus returned, a crowd welcomed him, for they were all expecting him. 41 Then a man named Jairus, a ruler of the synagogue, came and fell at Jesus' feet, pleading with him to come to his house 42 because his only daughter, a girl of about twelve, was dying.

As Jesus was on his way, the crowds almost crushed him. 43 And a woman was there who had been subject to bleeding for twelve years, but no one could heal her. 44 She came up behind him and touched the edge of his cloak, and immediately her bleeding stopped.

45 "Who touched me?" Jesus asked.

When they all denied it, Peter said, "Master, the people are crowding and pressing against you."

46 But Jesus said, "Someone touched me; I know that power has gone out from me."

47 Then the woman, seeing that she could not go unnoticed, came trembling and fell at his feet. In the presence of all the people, she told why she had touched him and how she had been instantly healed. 48 Then he said to her, "Daughter, your faith has healed you. Go in peace."

49 While Jesus was still speaking, someone came from the house of Jairus, the synagogue ruler. "Your daughter is dead," he said. "Don't bother the teacher any more."

50 Hearing this, Jesus said to Jairus, "Don't be afraid; just believe, and she will be healed."

51 When he arrived at the house of Jairus, he did not let anyone go in with him except Peter, John and James, and the child's father and mother. 52 Meanwhile, all the people were wailing and mourning for her. "Stop wailing," Jesus said. "She is not dead but asleep."

53 They laughed at him, knowing that she was dead. 54 But he took her by the hand and said, "My child, get up!" 55 Her spirit returned, and at once she stood up. Then Jesus told them to give her something

to eat. [56] Her parents were astonished, but he ordered them not to tell anyone what had happened.

DAY 13: "YOU ARE THE CHRIST OF GOD"—LUKE 9:1-36

CHAPTER 9

Jesus Sends Out the Twelve

[1] When Jesus had called the Twelve together, he gave them power and authority to drive out all demons and to cure diseases, [2] and he sent them out to preach the kingdom of God and to heal the sick. [3] He told them: "Take nothing for the journey—no staff, no bag, no bread, no money, no extra tunic. [4] Whatever house you enter, stay there until you leave that town. [5] If people do not welcome you, shake the dust off your feet when you leave their town, as a testimony against them." So they set out and went from village to village, preaching the Gospel and healing people everywhere.

[7] Now Herod the tetrarch heard about all that was going on. And he was perplexed, because some were saying that John had been raised from the dead, [8] others that Elijah had appeared, and still others that one of the prophets of long ago had come back to life. [9] But Herod said, "I beheaded John. Who, then, is this I hear such things about?" And he tried to see him.

Jesus Feeds the Five Thousand

[10] When the apostles returned, they reported to Jesus what they had done. Then he took them with him and they withdrew by themselves to a town called Bethsaida, [11] but the crowds learned about it and followed him. He welcomed them and spoke to them about the kingdom of God, and healed those who needed healing.

[12] Late in the afternoon the Twelve came to him and said, "Send the crowd away so they can go to the surrounding villages and countryside and find food and lodging, because we are in a remote place here."

13 He replied, "You give them something to eat."

They answered, "We have only five loaves of bread and two fish—unless we go and buy food for all this crowd." 14 (About five thousand men were there.)

But he said to his disciples, "Have them sit down in groups of about fifty each." 15 The disciples did so, and everybody sat down. 16Taking the five loaves and the two fish and looking up to heaven, he gave thanks and broke them. Then he gave them to the disciples to set before the people. 17 They all ate and were satisfied, and the disciples picked up twelve basketfuls of broken pieces that were left over.

Peter's Confession of Christ

18 Once when Jesus was praying in private and his disciples were with him, he asked them, "Who do the crowds say I am?"

19 They replied, "Some say John the Baptist; others say Elijah; and still others, that one of the prophets of long ago has come back to life."

20 "But what about you?" he asked. "Who do you say I am?"

Peter answered, "The Christ of God."

21 Jesus strictly warned them not to tell this to anyone. 22 And he said, "The Son of Man must suffer many things and be rejected by the elders, chief priests and teachers of the law, and he must be killed and on the third day be raised to life."

23 Then he said to them all: "If anyone would come after me, he must deny himself and take up his cross daily and follow me. 24 For whoever wants to save his life will lose it, but whoever loses his life for me will save it. 25 What good is it for a man to gain the whole world, and yet lose or forfeit his very self? 26 If anyone is ashamed of me and my words, the Son of Man will be ashamed of him when he comes in his glory and in the glory of the Father and of the holy angels. 27 I tell you the truth, some who are standing here will not taste death before they see the kingdom of God."

▼

The Transfiguration

28 About eight days after Jesus said this, he took Peter, John and James with him and went up onto a mountain to pray. 29 As he was praying, the appearance of his face changed, and his clothes became as bright as a flash of lightning. 30 Two men, Moses and Elijah, 31appeared in glorious splendor, talking with Jesus. They spoke about his departure, which he was about to bring to fulfillment at Jerusalem. 32 Peter and his companions were very sleepy, but when they became fully awake, they saw his glory and the two men standing with him. 33 As the men were leaving Jesus, Peter said to him, "Master, it is good for us to be here. Let us put up three shelters—one for you, one for Moses and one for Elijah." (He did not know what he was saying.)

34 While he was speaking, a cloud appeared and enveloped them, and they were afraid as they entered the cloud. 35 A voice came from the cloud, saying, "This is my Son, whom I have chosen; listen to him." 36 When the voice had spoken, they found that Jesus was alone. The disciples kept this to themselves, and told no one at that time what they had seen.

DAY 14: TRUE GREATNESS—LUKE 9:37-50

The Healing of a Boy with an Evil Spirit

37 The next day, when they came down from the mountain, a large crowd met him. 38 A man in the crowd called out, "Teacher, I beg you to look at my son, for he is my only child. 39 A spirit seizes him and he suddenly screams; it throws him into convulsions so that he foams at the mouth. It scarcely ever leaves him and is destroying him. 40 I begged your disciples to drive it out, but they could not."

41 "O unbelieving and perverse generation," Jesus replied, "how long shall I stay with you and put up with you? Bring your son here."

42 Even while the boy was coming, the demon threw him to the ground in a convulsion. But Jesus rebuked the evil spirit, healed the boy and gave him back to his father. 43 And they were all amazed at the greatness of God.

While everyone was marveling at all that Jesus did, he said to his disciples, 44 "Listen carefully to what I am about to tell you: The Son of Man is going to be betrayed into the hands of men." 45 But they did not understand what this meant. It was hidden from them, so that they did not grasp it, and they were afraid to ask him about it.

Who Will Be the Greatest?

46 An argument started among the disciples as to which of them would be the greatest. 47 Jesus, knowing their thoughts, took a little child and had him stand beside him. 48 Then he said to them, "Whoever welcomes this little child in my name welcomes me; and whoever welcomes me welcomes the one who sent me. For he who is least among you all—he is the greatest."

49 "Master," said John, "we saw a man driving out demons in your name and we tried to stop him, because he is not one of us."

50 "Do not stop him," Jesus said, "for whoever is not against you is for you."

DAY 15: WORKING FOR GOD'S KINGDOM—LUKE 9:51–10:24

Samaritan Opposition

51 As the time approached for him to be taken up to heaven, Jesus resolutely set out for Jerusalem. 52 And he sent messengers on ahead, who went into a Samaritan village to get things ready for him; 53 but the people there did not welcome him, because he was heading for Jerusalem. 54 When the disciples James and John saw this, they asked, "Lord, do you want us to call fire down from heaven to destroy them?" 55 But Jesus turned and rebuked them, 56 and they went to another village.

The Cost of Following Jesus

⁵⁷ As they were walking along the road, a man said to him, "I will follow you wherever you go."

⁵⁸ Jesus replied, "Foxes have holes and birds of the air have nests, but the Son of Man has no place to lay his head."

⁵⁹ He said to another man, "Follow me."

But the man replied, "Lord, first let me go and bury my father."

⁶⁰ Jesus said to him, "Let the dead bury their own dead, but you go and proclaim the kingdom of God."

⁶¹ Still another said, "I will follow you, Lord; but first let me go back and say good-by to my family."

⁶² Jesus replied, "No one who puts his hand to the plow and looks back is fit for service in the kingdom of God."

CHAPTER 10

Jesus Sends Out the Seventy-two

¹ After this the Lord appointed seventy-two others and sent them two by two ahead of him to every town and place where he was about to go. ² He told them, "The harvest is plentiful, but the workers are few. Ask the Lord of the harvest, therefore, to send out workers into his harvest field. ³ Go! I am sending you out like lambs among wolves. ⁴Do not take a purse or bag or sandals; and do not greet anyone on the road.

⁵ "When you enter a house, first say, 'Peace to this house.' ⁶ If a man of peace is there, your peace will rest on him; if not, it will return to you. ⁷ Stay in that house, eating and drinking whatever they give you, for the worker deserves his wages. Do not move around from house to house.

⁸ "When you enter a town and are welcomed, eat what is set before you. ⁹ Heal the sick who are there and tell them, 'The kingdom of God is near you.' ¹⁰ But when you enter a town and are not wel-

comed, go into its streets and say, [11] 'Even the dust of your town that sticks to our feet we wipe off against you. Yet be sure of this: The kingdom of God is near.' [12] I tell you, it will be more bearable on that day for Sodom than for that town.

[13] "Woe to you, Korazin! Woe to you, Bethsaida! For if the miracles that were performed in you had been performed in Tyre and Sidon, they would have repented long ago, sitting in sackcloth and ashes. [14]But it will be more bearable for Tyre and Sidon at the judgment than for you. [15] And you, Capernaum, will you be lifted up to the skies? No, you will go down to the depths.

[16] "He who listens to you listens to me; he who rejects you rejects me; but he who rejects me rejects him who sent me."

[17] The seventy-two returned with joy and said, "Lord, even the demons submit to us in your name."

[18] He replied, "I saw Satan fall like lightning from heaven. [19] I have given you authority to trample on snakes and scorpions and to overcome all the power of the enemy; nothing will harm you. [20] However, do not rejoice that the spirits submit to you, but rejoice that your names are written in heaven."

[21] At that time Jesus, full of joy through the Holy Spirit, said, "I praise you, Father, Lord of heaven and earth, because you have hidden these things from the wise and learned, and revealed them to little children. Yes, Father, for this was your good pleasure.

[22] "All things have been committed to me by my Father. No one knows who the Son is except the Father, and no one knows who the Father is except the Son and those to whom the Son chooses to reveal him."

[23] Then he turned to his disciples and said privately, "Blessed are the eyes that see what you see. [24] For I tell you that many prophets and kings wanted to see what you see but did not see it, and to hear what you hear but did not hear it."

DAY 16: "LOVE YOUR NEIGHBOR"—LUKE 10:25–11:13

The Parable of the Good Samaritan

25 On one occasion an expert in the law stood up to test Jesus. "Teacher," he asked, "what must I do to inherit eternal life?"

26 "What is written in the Law?" he replied. "How do you read it?"

27 He answered: "'Love the Lord your God with all your heart and with all your soul and with all your strength and with all your mind'; and, 'Love your neighbor as yourself.'"

28 "You have answered correctly," Jesus replied. "Do this and you will live."

29 But he wanted to justify himself, so he asked Jesus, "And who is my neighbor?"

30 In reply Jesus said: "A man was going down from Jerusalem to Jericho, when he fell into the hands of robbers. They stripped him of his clothes, beat him and went away, leaving him half dead. 31 A priest happened to be going down the same road, and when he saw the man, he passed by on the other side. 32 So too, a Levite, when he came to the place and saw him, passed by on the other side. 33 But a Samaritan, as he traveled, came where the man was; and when he saw him, he took pity on him. 34 He went to him and bandaged his wounds, pouring on oil and wine. Then he put the man on his own donkey, took him to an inn and took care of him. 35 The next day he took out two silver coins and gave them to the innkeeper. 'Look after him,' he said, 'and when I return, I will reimburse you for any extra expense you may have.'

36 "Which of these three do you think was a neighbor to the man who fell into the hands of robbers?"

37 The expert in the law replied, "The one who had mercy on him." Jesus told him, "Go and do likewise."

At the Home of Martha and Mary

38 As Jesus and his disciples were on their way, he came to a village where a woman named Martha opened her home to him. 39 She

had a sister called Mary, who sat at the Lord's feet listening to what he said. 40 But Martha was distracted by all the preparations that had to be made. She came to him and asked, "Lord, don't you care that my sister has left me to do the work by myself? Tell her to help me!"

41 "Martha, Martha," the Lord answered, "you are worried and upset about many things, 42 but only one thing is needed. Mary has chosen what is better, and it will not be taken away from her."

CHAPTER 11

Jesus' Teaching on Prayer

1 One day Jesus was praying in a certain place. When he finished, one of his disciples said to him, "Lord, teach us to pray, just as John taught his disciples."

2 He said to them, "When you pray, say: 'Father, hallowed be your name, your kingdom come. 3 Give us each day our daily bread. 4Forgive us our sins, for we also forgive everyone who sins against us. And lead us not into temptation.'"

5 Then he said to them, "Suppose one of you has a friend, and he goes to him at midnight and says, 'Friend, lend me three loaves of bread, 6 because a friend of mine on a journey has come to me, and I have nothing to set before him.'

7 "Then the one inside answers, 'Don't bother me. The door is already locked, and my children are with me in bed. I can't get up and give you anything.' 8 I tell you, though he will not get up and give him the bread because he is his friend, yet because of the man's persistence he will get up and give him as much as he needs.

9 "So I say to you: Ask and it will be given to you; seek and you will find; knock and the door will be opened to you. 10 For everyone who asks receives; he who seeks finds; and to him who knocks, the door will be opened.

11 "Which of you fathers, if your son asks for a fish, will give him a snake instead? 12 Or if he asks for an egg, will give him a scorpion?

▼

¹³ If you then, though you are evil, know how to give good gifts to your children, how much more will your Father in heaven give the Holy Spirit to those who ask him!"

DAY 17: LIVING AS GOD'S PEOPLE—LUKE 11:14-54

Jesus and Beelzebub

¹⁴ Jesus was driving out a demon that was mute. When the demon left, the man who had been mute spoke, and the crowd was amazed. ¹⁵ But some of them said, "By Beelzebub, the prince of demons, he is driving out demons." ¹⁶ Others tested him by asking for a sign from heaven.

¹⁷ Jesus knew their thoughts and said to them: "Any kingdom divided against itself will be ruined, and a house divided against itself will fall. ¹⁸ If Satan is divided against himself, how can his kingdom stand? I say this because you claim that I drive out demons by Beelzebub. ¹⁹ Now if I drive out demons by Beelzebub, by whom do your followers drive them out? So then, they will be your judges. ²⁰ But if I drive out demons by the finger of God, then the kingdom of God has come to you.

²¹ "When a strong man, fully armed, guards his own house, his possessions are safe. ²² But when someone stronger attacks and overpowers him, he takes away the armor in which the man trusted and divides up the spoils.

²³ "He who is not with me is against me, and he who does not gather with me, scatters.

²⁴ "When an evil spirit comes out of a man, it goes through arid places seeking rest and does not find it. Then it says, 'I will return to the house I left.' ²⁵ When it arrives, it finds the house swept clean and put in order. ²⁶ Then it goes and takes seven other spirits more wicked than itself, and they go in and live there. And the final condition of that man is worse than the first."

27 As Jesus was saying these things, a woman in the crowd called out, "Blessed is the mother who gave you birth and nursed you."

28 He replied, "Blessed rather are those who hear the word of God and obey it."

The Sign of Jonah

29 As the crowds increased, Jesus said, "This is a wicked generation. It asks for a miraculous sign, but none will be given it except the sign of Jonah. 30 For as Jonah was a sign to the Ninevites, so also will the Son of Man be to this generation. 31 The Queen of the South will rise at the judgment with the men of this generation and condemn them; for she came from the ends of the earth to listen to Solomon's wisdom, and now one greater than Solomon is here. 32 The men of Nineveh will stand up at the judgment with this generation and condemn it, for they repented at the preaching of Jonah, and now one greater than Jonah is here."

The Lamp of the Body

33 "No one lights a lamp and puts it in a place where it will be hidden, or under a bowl. Instead he puts it on its stand, so that those who come in may see the light. 34 Your eye is the lamp of your body. When your eyes are good, your whole body also is full of light. But when they are bad, your body also is full of darkness. 35 See to it, then, that the light within you is not darkness. 36 Therefore, if your whole body is full of light, and no part of it dark, it will be completely lighted, as when the light of a lamp shines on you."

Six Woes

37 When Jesus had finished speaking, a Pharisee invited him to eat with him; so he went in and reclined at the table. 38 But the Pharisee, noticing that Jesus did not first wash before the meal, was surprised.

39 Then the Lord said to him, "Now then, you Pharisees clean the

outside of the cup and dish, but inside you are full of greed and wickedness. [40] You foolish people! Did not the one who made the outside make the inside also? [41] But give what is inside the dish to the poor, and everything will be clean for you.

[42] "Woe to you Pharisees, because you give God a tenth of your mint, rue and all other kinds of garden herbs, but you neglect justice and the love of God. You should have practiced the latter without leaving the former undone.

[43] "Woe to you Pharisees, because you love the most important seats in the synagogues and greetings in the marketplaces.

[44] "Woe to you, because you are like unmarked graves, which men walk over without knowing it."

[45] One of the experts in the law answered him, "Teacher, when you say these things, you insult us also."

[46] Jesus replied, "And you experts in the law, woe to you, because you load people down with burdens they can hardly carry, and you yourselves will not lift one finger to help them.

[47] "Woe to you, because you build tombs for the prophets, and it was your forefathers who killed them. [48] So you testify that you approve of what your forefathers did; they killed the prophets, and you build their tombs. [49] Because of this, God in his wisdom said, 'I will send them prophets and apostles, some of whom they will kill and others they will persecute.' [50] Therefore this generation will be held responsible for the blood of all the prophets that has been shed since the beginning of the world, [51] from the blood of Abel to the blood of Zechariah, who was killed between the altar and the sanctuary. Yes, I tell you, this generation will be held responsible for it all.

[52] "Woe to you experts in the law, because you have taken away the key to knowledge. You yourselves have not entered, and you have hindered those who were entering."

[53] When Jesus left there, the Pharisees and the teachers of the law

began to oppose him fiercely and to besiege him with questions, 54waiting to catch him in something he might say.

DAY 18: BE PREPARED—LUKE 12:1-59

CHAPTER 12

Warnings and Encouragements

1 Meanwhile, when a crowd of many thousands had gathered, so that they were trampling on one another, Jesus began to speak first to his disciples, saying: "Be on your guard against the yeast of the Pharisees, which is hypocrisy. 2 There is nothing concealed that will not be disclosed, or hidden that will not be made known. 3 What you have said in the dark will be heard in the daylight, and what you have whispered in the ear in the inner rooms will be proclaimed from the housetops.

4 "I tell you, my friends, do not be afraid of those who kill the body and after that can do no more. 5 But I will show you whom you should fear: Fear him who, after the killing of the body, has power to throw you into hell. Yes, I tell you, fear him. 6 Are not five sparrows sold for two pennies? Yet not one of them is forgotten by God. 7 Indeed, the very hairs of your head are all numbered. Don't be afraid; you are worth more than many sparrows.

8 "I tell you, whoever acknowledges me before men, the Son of Man will also acknowledge him before the angels of God. 9 But he who disowns me before men will be disowned before the angels of God. 10And everyone who speaks a word against the Son of Man will be forgiven, but anyone who blasphemes against the Holy Spirit will not be forgiven.

11 "When you are brought before synagogues, rulers and authorities, do not worry about how you will defend yourselves or what you will say, 12 for the Holy Spirit will teach you at that time what you should say."

The Parable of the Rich Fool

13 Someone in the crowd said to him, "Teacher, tell my brother to divide the inheritance with me."

14 Jesus replied, "Man, who appointed me a judge or an arbiter between you?" 15 Then he said to them, "Watch out! Be on your guard against all kinds of greed; a man's life does not consist in the abundance of his possessions."

16 And he told them this parable: "The ground of a certain rich man produced a good crop. 17 He thought to himself, 'What shall I do? I have no place to store my crops.'

18 "Then he said, 'This is what I'll do. I will tear down my barns and build bigger ones, and there I will store all my grain and my goods. 19 And I'll say to myself, "You have plenty of good things laid up for many years. Take life easy; eat, drink and be merry."'

20 "But God said to him, 'You fool! This very night your life will be demanded from you. Then who will get what you have prepared for yourself?'

21 "This is how it will be with anyone who stores up things for himself but is not rich toward God."

"Do Not Worry"

22 Then Jesus said to his disciples: "Therefore I tell you, do not worry about your life, what you will eat; or about your body, what you will wear. 23 Life is more than food, and the body more than clothes. 24 Consider the ravens: They do not sow or reap, they have no storeroom or barn; yet God feeds them. And how much more valuable you are than birds! 25 Who of you by worrying can add a single hour to his life? 26 Since you cannot do this very little thing, why do you worry about the rest?

27 "Consider how the lilies grow. They do not labor or spin. Yet I tell you, not even Solomon in all his splendor was dressed like one of these. 28 If that is how God clothes the grass of the field, which is here

today, and tomorrow is thrown into the fire, how much more will he clothe you, O you of little faith! 29 And do not set your heart on what you will eat or drink; do not worry about it. 30 For the pagan world runs after all such things, and your Father knows that you need them. 31 But seek his kingdom, and these things will be given to you as well.

32 "Do not be afraid, little flock, for your Father has been pleased to give you the kingdom. 33 Sell your possessions and give to the poor. Provide purses for yourselves that will not wear out, a treasure in heaven that will not be exhausted, where no thief comes near and no moth destroys. 34 For where your treasure is, there your heart will be also."

Watchfulness

35 "Be dressed ready for service and keep your lamps burning, 36like men waiting for their master to return from a wedding banquet, so that when he comes and knocks they can immediately open the door for him. 37 It will be good for those servants whose master finds them watching when he comes. I tell you the truth, he will dress himself to serve, will have them recline at the table and will come and wait on them. 38 It will be good for those servants whose master finds them ready, even if he comes in the second or third watch of the night. 39 But understand this: If the owner of the house had known at what hour the thief was coming, he would not have let his house be broken into. 40 You also must be ready, because the Son of Man will come at an hour when you do not expect him."

41 Peter asked, "Lord, are you telling this parable to us, or to everyone?"

42 The Lord answered, "Who then is the faithful and wise manager, whom the master puts in charge of his servants to give them their food allowance at the proper time? 43 It will be good for that servant whom the master finds doing so when he returns. 44 I tell you the truth, he will put him in charge of all his possessions. 45 But suppose

▼

the servant says to himself, 'My master is taking a long time in coming,' and he then begins to beat the menservants and maidservants
and to eat and drink and get drunk. [46] The master of that servant will
come on a day when he does not expect him and at an hour he is not
aware of. He will cut him to pieces and assign him a place with the
unbelievers.

[47] "That servant who knows his master's will and does not get
ready or does not do what his master wants will be beaten with many
blows. [48] But the one who does not know and does things deserving
punishment will be beaten with few blows. From everyone who has
been given much, much will be demanded; and from the one who
has been entrusted with much, much more will be asked."

Not Peace but Division

[49] "I have come to bring fire on the earth, and how I wish it were
already kindled! [50] But I have a baptism to undergo, and how dis-
tressed I am until it is completed! [51] Do you think I came to bring
peace on earth? No, I tell you, but division. [52] From now on there will
be five in one family divided against each other, three against two and
two against three. [53] They will be divided, father against son and son
against father, mother against daughter and daughter against
mother, mother-in-law against daughter-in-law and daughter-in-law
against mother-in-law."

Interpreting the Times

[54] He said to the crowd: "When you see a cloud rising in the west,
immediately you say, 'It's going to rain,' and it does. [55] And when the
south wind blows, you say, 'It's going to be hot,' and it is.
[56]Hypocrites! You know how to interpret the appearance of the earth
and the sky. How is it that you don't know how to interpret this present time?

[57] "Why don't you judge for yourselves what is right? [58] As you are
going with your adversary to the magistrate, try hard to be reconciled

to him on the way, or he may drag you off to the judge, and the judge turn you over to the officer, and the officer throw you into prison. 59 I tell you, you will not get out until you have paid the last penny."

DAY 19: ENTER THROUGH THE NARROW DOOR—LUKE 13:1-35

CHAPTER 13

Repent or Perish

1 Now there were some present at that time who told Jesus about the Galileans whose blood Pilate had mixed with their sacrifices. 2Jesus answered, "Do you think that these Galileans were worse sinners than all the other Galileans because they suffered this way? 3 I tell you, no! But unless you repent, you too will all perish. 4 Or those eighteen who died when the tower in Siloam fell on them—do you think they were more guilty than all the others living in Jerusalem? 5 I tell you, no! But unless you repent, you too will all perish."

6 Then he told this parable: "A man had a fig tree, planted in his vineyard, and he went to look for fruit on it, but did not find any. 7 So he said to the man who took care of the vineyard, 'For three years now I've been coming to look for fruit on this fig tree and haven't found any. Cut it down! Why should it use up the soil?'

8 "'Sir,' the man replied, 'leave it alone for one more year, and I'll dig around it and fertilize it. 9 If it bears fruit next year, fine! If not, then cut it down.'"

A Crippled Woman Healed on the Sabbath

10 On a Sabbath Jesus was teaching in one of the synagogues, 11and a woman was there who had been crippled by a spirit for eighteen years. She was bent over and could not straighten up at all. 12When Jesus saw her, he called her forward and said to her, "Woman, you are set free from your infirmity." 13 Then he put his hands on her, and immediately she straightened up and praised God.

14 Indignant because Jesus had healed on the Sabbath, the synagogue ruler said to the people, "There are six days for work. So come and be healed on those days, not on the Sabbath."

15 The Lord answered him, "You hypocrites! Doesn't each of you on the Sabbath untie his ox or donkey from the stall and lead it out to give it water? 16 Then should not this woman, a daughter of Abraham, whom Satan has kept bound for eighteen long years, be set free on the Sabbath day from what bound her?"

17 When he said this, all his opponents were humiliated, but the people were delighted with all the wonderful things he was doing.

The Parables of the Mustard Seed and the Yeast

18 Then Jesus asked, "What is the kingdom of God like? What shall I compare it to? 19 It is like a mustard seed, which a man took and planted in his garden. It grew and became a tree, and the birds of the air perched in its branches."

20 Again he asked, "What shall I compare the kingdom of God to? 21 It is like yeast that a woman took and mixed into a large amount of flour until it worked all through the dough."

The Narrow Door

22 Then Jesus went through the towns and villages, teaching as he made his way to Jerusalem. 23 Someone asked him, "Lord, are only a few people going to be saved?"

He said to them, 24 "Make every effort to enter through the narrow door, because many, I tell you, will try to enter and will not be able to. 25 Once the owner of the house gets up and closes the door, you will stand outside knocking and pleading, 'Sir, open the door for us.'

"But he will answer, 'I don't know you or where you come from.'

26 "Then you will say, 'We ate and drank with you, and you taught in our streets.'

27 "But he will reply, 'I don't know you or where you come from. Away from me, all you evildoers!'

28 "There will be weeping there, and gnashing of teeth, when you see Abraham, Isaac and Jacob and all the prophets in the kingdom of God, but you yourselves thrown out. 29 People will come from east and west and north and south, and will take their places at the feast in the kingdom of God. 30 Indeed there are those who are last who will be first, and first who will be last."

Jesus' Sorrow for Jerusalem

31 At that time some Pharisees came to Jesus and said to him, "Leave this place and go somewhere else. Herod wants to kill you."

32 He replied, "Go tell that fox, I will drive out demons and heal people today and tomorrow, and on the third day I will reach my goal. 33 In any case, I must keep going today and tomorrow and the next day—for surely no prophet can die outside Jerusalem!

34 "O Jerusalem, Jerusalem, you who kill the prophets and stone those sent to you, how often I have longed to gather your children together, as a hen gathers her chicks under her wings, but you were not willing! 35 Look, your house is left to you desolate. I tell you, you will not see me again until you say, 'Blessed is he who comes in the name of the Lord.'"

DAY 20: THE COST OF BEING A DISCIPLE—LUKE 14:1-35

CHAPTER 14

Jesus at a Pharisee's House

1 One Sabbath, when Jesus went to eat in the house of a prominent Pharisee, he was being carefully watched. 2 There in front of him was a man suffering from dropsy. 3 Jesus asked the Pharisees and experts in the law, "Is it lawful to heal on the Sabbath or not?" 4 But they remained silent. So taking hold of the man, he healed him and sent him away.

5 Then he asked them, "If one of you has a son or an ox that falls

into a well on the Sabbath day, will you not immediately pull him out?" 6 And they had nothing to say.

7 When he noticed how the guests picked the places of honor at the table, he told them this parable: 8 "When someone invites you to a wedding feast, do not take the place of honor, for a person more distinguished than you may have been invited. 9 If so, the host who invited both of you will come and say to you, 'Give this man your seat.' Then, humiliated, you will have to take the least important place. 10 But when you are invited, take the lowest place, so that when your host comes, he will say to you, 'Friend, move up to a better place.' Then you will be honored in the presence of all your fellow guests. 11 For everyone who exalts himself will be humbled, and he who humbles himself will be exalted."

12 Then Jesus said to his host, "When you give a luncheon or dinner, do not invite your friends, your brothers or relatives, or your rich neighbors; if you do, they may invite you back and so you will be repaid. 13 But when you give a banquet, invite the poor, the crippled, the lame, the blind, 14 and you will be blessed. Although they cannot repay you, you will be repaid at the resurrection of the righteous."

The Parable of the Great Banquet

15 When one of those at the table with him heard this, he said to Jesus, "Blessed is the man who will eat at the feast in the kingdom of God."

16 Jesus replied: "A certain man was preparing a great banquet and invited many guests. 17 At the time of the banquet he sent his servant to tell those who had been invited, 'Come, for everything is now ready.'

18 "But they all alike began to make excuses. The first said, 'I have just bought a field, and I must go and see it. Please excuse me.'

19 "Another said, 'I have just bought five yoke of oxen, and I'm on my way to try them out. Please excuse me.'

20 "Still another said, 'I just got married, so I can't come.'

21 "The servant came back and reported this to his master. Then the owner of the house became angry and ordered his servant, 'Go out quickly into the streets and alleys of the town and bring in the poor, the crippled, the blind and the lame.'

22 "'Sir,' the servant said, 'what you ordered has been done, but there is still room.'

23 "Then the master told his servant, 'Go out to the roads and country lanes and make them come in, so that my house will be full. 24 I tell you, not one of those men who were invited will get a taste of my banquet.'"

The Cost of Being a Disciple of Christ

25 Large crowds were traveling with Jesus, and turning to them he said: 26 "If anyone comes to me and does not hate his father and mother, his wife and children, his brothers and sisters—yes, even his own life—he cannot be my disciple. 27 And anyone who does not carry his cross and follow me cannot be my disciple.

28 "Suppose one of you wants to build a tower. Will he not first sit down and estimate the cost to see if he has enough money to complete it? 29 For if he lays the foundation and is not able to finish it, everyone who sees it will ridicule him, 30 saying, 'This fellow began to build and was not able to finish.'

31 "Or suppose a king is about to go to war against another king. Will he not first sit down and consider whether he is able with ten thousand men to oppose the one coming against him with twenty thousand? 32 If he is not able, he will send a delegation while the other is still a long way off and will ask for terms of peace. 33 In the same way, any of you who does not give up everything he has cannot be my disciple.

34 "Salt is good, but if it loses its saltiness, how can it be made salty again? 35 It is fit neither for the soil nor for the manure pile; it is thrown out.

"He who has ears to hear, let him hear."

▼

DAY 21: LOST AND FOUND—LUKE 15:1-32

CHAPTER 15

The Parable of the Great Banquet

¹ Now the tax collectors and "sinners" were all gathering around to hear him. ² But the Pharisees and the teachers of the law muttered, "This man welcomes sinners and eats with them."

³ Then Jesus told them this parable: ⁴ "Suppose one of you has a hundred sheep and loses one of them. Does he not leave the ninety-nine in the open country and go after the lost sheep until he finds it? ⁵And when he finds it, he joyfully puts it on his shoulders ⁶ and goes home. Then he calls his friends and neighbors together and says, 'Rejoice with me; I have found my lost sheep.' ⁷ I tell you that in the same way there will be more rejoicing in heaven over one sinner who repents than over ninety-nine righteous persons who do not need to repent."

The Parable of the Lost Coin

⁸ "Or suppose a woman has ten silver coins and loses one. Does she not light a lamp, sweep the house and search carefully until she finds it? ⁹ And when she finds it, she calls her friends and neighbors together and says, 'Rejoice with me; I have found my lost coin.' ¹⁰ In the same way, I tell you, there is rejoicing in the presence of the angels of God over one sinner who repents."

The Parable of the Lost Son

¹¹ Jesus continued: "There was a man who had two sons. ¹² The younger one said to his father, 'Father, give me my share of the estate.' So he divided his property between them.

¹³ "Not long after that, the younger son got together all he had, set off for a distant country and there squandered his wealth in wild living. ¹⁴ After he had spent everything, there was a severe famine in that whole country, and he began to be in need. ¹⁵ So he went and hired himself out to a citizen of that country, who sent him to his fields to

feed pigs. 16 He longed to fill his stomach with the pods that the pigs were eating, but no one gave him anything.

17 "When he came to his senses, he said, 'How many of my father's hired men have food to spare, and here I am starving to death! 18 I will set out and go back to my father and say to him: "Father, I have sinned against heaven and against you. 19 I am no longer worthy to be called your son; make me like one of your hired men."' 20 So he got up and went to his father.

"But while he was still a long way off, his father saw him and was filled with compassion for him; he ran to his son, threw his arms around him and kissed him.

21 "The son said to him, 'Father, I have sinned against heaven and against you. I am no longer worthy to be called your son.'

22 "But the father said to his servants, 'Quick! Bring the best robe and put it on him. Put a ring on his finger and sandals on his feet. 23Bring the fattened calf and kill it. Let's have a feast and celebrate. 24For this son of mine was dead and is alive again; he was lost and is found.' So they began to celebrate.

25 "Meanwhile, the older son was in the field. When he came near the house, he heard music and dancing. 26 So he called one of the servants and asked him what was going on. 27 'Your brother has come,' he replied, 'and your father has killed the fattened calf because he has him back safe and sound.'

28 "The older brother became angry and refused to go in. So his father went out and pleaded with him. 29 But he answered his father, 'Look! All these years I've been slaving for you and never disobeyed your orders. Yet you never gave me even a young goat so I could celebrate with my friends. 30 But when this son of yours who has squandered your property with prostitutes comes home, you kill the fattened calf for him!'

31 "'My son,' the father said, 'you are always with me, and everything I have is yours. 32 But we had to celebrate and be glad, because

▼

this brother of yours was dead and is alive again; he was lost and is found.'"

DAY 22: "YOU CANNOT SERVE BOTH GOD AND MONEY"—LUKE 16:1-31

CHAPTER 16

The Parable of the Shrewd Manager

1 Jesus told his disciples: "There was a rich man whose manager was accused of wasting his possessions. 2 So he called him in and asked him, 'What is this I hear about you? Give an account of your management, because you cannot be manager any longer.'

3 "The manager said to himself, 'What shall I do now? My master is taking away my job. I'm not strong enough to dig, and I'm ashamed to beg— 4 I know what I'll do so that, when I lose my job here, people will welcome me into their houses.'

5 "So he called in each one of his master's debtors. He asked the first, 'How much do you owe my master?'

6 "'Eight hundred gallons of olive oil,' he replied.

"The manager told him, 'Take your bill, sit down quickly, and make it four hundred.'

7 "Then he asked the second, 'And how much do you owe?'

"'A thousand bushels of wheat,' he replied.

"He told him, 'Take your bill and make it eight hundred.'

8 "The master commended the dishonest manager because he had acted shrewdly. For the people of this world are more shrewd in dealing with their own kind than are the people of the light. 9 I tell you, use worldly wealth to gain friends for yourselves, so that when it is gone, you will be welcomed into eternal dwellings.

10 "Whoever can be trusted with very little can also be trusted with much, and whoever is dishonest with very little will also be dishonest with much. 11 So if you have not been trustworthy in handling

worldly wealth, who will trust you with true riches? 12 And if you have not been trustworthy with someone else's property, who will give you property of your own?

13 "No servant can serve two masters. Either he will hate the one and love the other, or he will be devoted to the one and despise the other. You cannot serve both God and Money."

14 The Pharisees, who loved money, heard all this and were sneering at Jesus. 15 He said to them, "You are the ones who justify yourselves in the eyes of men, but God knows your hearts. What is highly valued among men is detestable in God's sight.

16 "The Law and the Prophets were proclaimed until John. Since that time, the good news of the kingdom of God is being preached, and everyone is forcing his way into it. 17 It is easier for heaven and earth to disappear than for the least stroke of a pen to drop out of the Law.

18 "Anyone who divorces his wife and marries another woman commits adultery, and the man who marries a divorced woman commits adultery."

The Rich Man and Lazarus

19 "There was a rich man who was dressed in purple and fine linen and lived in luxury every day. 20 At his gate was laid a beggar named Lazarus, covered with sores 21 and longing to eat what fell from the rich man's table. Even the dogs came and licked his sores.

22 "The time came when the beggar died and the angels carried him to Abraham's side. The rich man also died and was buried. 23In hell, where he was in torment, he looked up and saw Abraham far away, with Lazarus by his side. 24 So he called to him, 'Father Abraham, have pity on me and send Lazarus to dip the tip of his finger in water and cool my tongue, because I am in agony in this fire.'

25 "But Abraham replied, 'Son, remember that in your lifetime you received your good things, while Lazarus received bad things, but

now he is comforted here and you are in agony. 26 And besides all this, between us and you a great chasm has been fixed, so that those who want to go from here to you cannot, nor can anyone cross over from there to us.'

27 "He answered, 'Then I beg you, father, send Lazarus to my father's house, 28 for I have five brothers. Let him warn them, so that they will not also come to this place of torment.'

29 "Abraham replied, 'They have Moses and the Prophets; let them listen to them.'

30 "'No, father Abraham,' he said, 'but if someone from the dead goes to them, they will repent.'

31 "He said to him, 'If they do not listen to Moses and the Prophets, they will not be convinced even if someone rises from the dead.'"

DAY 23: FORGIVENESS, FAITH, AND THE COMING KING—LUKE 17:1-37

CHAPTER 17

Sin, Faith, Duty

1 Jesus said to his disciples: "Things that cause people to sin are bound to come, but woe to that person through whom they come. 2 It would be better for him to be thrown into the sea with a millstone tied around his neck than for him to cause one of these little ones to sin. 3 So watch yourselves.

"If your brother sins, rebuke him, and if he repents, forgive him. 4 If he sins against you seven times in a day, and seven times comes back to you and says, 'I repent,' forgive him."

5 The apostles said to the Lord, "Increase our faith!"

6 He replied, "If you have faith as small as a mustard seed, you can say to this mulberry tree, 'Be uprooted and planted in the sea,' and it will obey you.

7 "Suppose one of you had a servant plowing or looking after the

sheep. Would he say to the servant when he comes in from the field, 'Come along now and sit down to eat'? 8 Would he not rather say, 'Prepare my supper, get yourself ready and wait on me while I eat and drink; after that you may eat and drink'? 9 Would he thank the servant because he did what he was told to do? 10 So you also, when you have done everything you were told to do, should say, 'We are unworthy servants; we have only done our duty.'"

Ten Healed of Leprosy

11 Now on his way to Jerusalem, Jesus traveled along the border between Samaria and Galilee. 12 As he was going into a village, ten men who had leprosy met him. They stood at a distance 13 and called out in a loud voice, "Jesus, Master, have pity on us!"

14 When he saw them, he said, "Go, show yourselves to the priests." And as they went, they were cleansed.

15 One of them, when he saw he was healed, came back, praising God in a loud voice. 16 He threw himself at Jesus' feet and thanked him—and he was a Samaritan.

17 Jesus asked, "Were not all ten cleansed? Where are the other nine? 18 Was no one found to return and give praise to God except this foreigner?" 19 Then he said to him, "Rise and go; your faith has made you well."

The Coming of the Kingdom of God

20 Once, having been asked by the Pharisees when the kingdom of God would come, Jesus replied, "The kingdom of God does not come visibly, 21 nor will people say, 'Here it is,' or 'There it is,' because the kingdom of God is within you."

22 Then he said to his disciples, "The time is coming when you will long to see one of the days of the Son of Man, but you will not see it. 23 Men will tell you, 'There he is!' or 'Here he is!' Do not go running off after them. 24 For the Son of Man in his day will be like the lightning,

which flashes and lights up the sky from one end to the other. 25 But first he must suffer many things and be rejected by this generation.

26 "Just as it was in the days of Noah, so also will it be in the days of the Son of Man. 27 People were eating, drinking, marrying and being given in marriage up to the day Noah entered the ark. Then the flood came and destroyed them all.

28 "It was the same in the days of Lot. People were eating and drinking, buying and selling, planting and building. 29 But the day Lot left Sodom, fire and sulfur rained down from heaven and destroyed them all.

30 "It will be just like this on the day the Son of Man is revealed. 31On that day no one who is on the roof of his house, with his goods inside, should go down to get them. Likewise, no one in the field should go back for anything. 32 Remember Lot's wife! 33 Whoever tries to keep his life will lose it, and whoever loses his life will preserve it. 34 I tell you, on that night two people will be in one bed; one will be taken and the other left. 35 Two women will be grinding grain together; one will be taken and the other left."

37 "Where, Lord?" they asked.

He replied, "Where there is a dead body, there the vultures will gather."

DAY 24: RECEIVE THE KINGDOM OF GOD LIKE A LITTLE CHILD—LUKE 18:1-43

CHAPTER 18

The Parable of the Persistent Widow

1 Then Jesus told his disciples a parable to show them that they should always pray and not give up. 2 He said: "In a certain town there was a judge who neither feared God nor cared about men. 3 And there was a widow in that town who kept coming to him with the plea, 'Grant me justice against my adversary.'

4 "For some time he refused. But finally he said to himself, 'Even though I don't fear God or care about men, 5 yet because this widow keeps bothering me, I will see that she gets justice, so that she won't eventually wear me out with her coming!'"

6 And the Lord said, "Listen to what the unjust judge says. 7 And will not God bring about justice for his chosen ones, who cry out to him day and night? Will he keep putting them off? 8 I tell you, he will see that they get justice, and quickly. However, when the Son of Man comes, will he find faith on the earth?"

The Parable of the Pharisee and the Tax Collector

9 To some who were confident of their own righteousness and looked down on everybody else, Jesus told this parable: 10 "Two men went up to the temple to pray, one a Pharisee and the other a tax collector. 11 The Pharisee stood up and prayed about himself: 'God, I thank you that I am not like other men—robbers, evildoers, adulterers—or even like this tax collector. 12 I fast twice a week and give a tenth of all my income.'

13 "But the tax collector stood at a distance. He would not even look up to heaven, but beat his breast and said, 'God, have mercy on me, a sinner.'

14 "I tell you that this man, rather than the other, went home justified before God. For everyone who exalts himself will be humbled, and he who humbles himself will be exalted."

The Little Children and Jesus

15 People were also bringing babies to Jesus to have him touch them. When the disciples saw this, they rebuked them. 16 But Jesus called the children to him and said, "Let the little children come to me, and do not hinder them, for the kingdom of God belongs to such as these. 17 I tell you the truth, anyone who will not receive the kingdom of God like a little child will never enter it."

The Rich Ruler

18 A certain ruler asked him, "Good teacher, what must I do to inherit eternal life?"

19 "Why do you call me good?" Jesus answered. "No one is good—except God alone. 20 You know the commandments: 'Do not commit adultery, do not murder, do not steal, do not give false testimony, honor your father and mother.'"

21 "All these I have kept since I was a boy," he said.

22 When Jesus heard this, he said to him, "You still lack one thing. Sell everything you have and give to the poor, and you will have treasure in heaven. Then come, follow me."

23 When he heard this, he became very sad, because he was a man of great wealth. 24 Jesus looked at him and said, "How hard it is for the rich to enter the kingdom of God! 25 Indeed, it is easier for a camel to go through the eye of a needle than for a rich man to enter the kingdom of God."

26 Those who heard this asked, "Who then can be saved?"

27 Jesus replied, "What is impossible with men is possible with God."

28 Peter said to him, "We have left all we had to follow you!"

29 "I tell you the truth," Jesus said to them, "no one who has left home or wife or brothers or parents or children for the sake of the kingdom of God 30 will fail to receive many times as much in this age and, in the age to come, eternal life."

Jesus Again Predicts His Death

31 Jesus took the Twelve aside and told them, "We are going up to Jerusalem, and everything that is written by the prophets about the Son of Man will be fulfilled. 32 He will be handed over to the Gentiles. They will mock him, insult him, spit on him, flog him and kill him. 33On the third day he will rise again."

34 The disciples did not understand any of this. Its meaning was

hidden from them, and they did not know what he was talking about.

A Blind Beggar Receives His Sight

35 As Jesus approached Jericho, a blind man was sitting by the roadside begging. 36 When he heard the crowd going by, he asked what was happening. 37 They told him, "Jesus of Nazareth is passing by."

38 He called out, "Jesus, Son of David, have mercy on me!"

39 Those who led the way rebuked him and told him to be quiet, but he shouted all the more, "Son of David, have mercy on me!"

40 Jesus stopped and ordered the man to be brought to him. When he came near, Jesus asked him, 41 "What do you want me to do for you?"

"Lord, I want to see," he replied.

42 Jesus said to him, "Receive your sight; your faith has healed you." 43 Immediately he received his sight and followed Jesus, praising God. When all the people saw it, they also praised God.

DAY 25: THE KING IS HERE—LUKE 19:1-48

CHAPTER 19

Zacchaeus the Tax Collector

1 Jesus entered Jericho and was passing through. 2 A man was there by the name of Zacchaeus; he was a chief tax collector and was wealthy. 3 He wanted to see who Jesus was, but being a short man he could not, because of the crowd. 4 So he ran ahead and climbed a sycamore-fig tree to see him, since Jesus was coming that way.

5 When Jesus reached the spot, he looked up and said to him, "Zacchaeus, come down immediately. I must stay at your house today." 6 So he came down at once and welcomed him gladly.

7 All the people saw this and began to mutter, "He has gone to be the guest of a 'sinner.'"

8 But Zacchaeus stood up and said to the Lord, "Look, Lord! Here

and now I give half of my possessions to the poor, and if I have cheated anybody out of anything, I will pay back four times the amount."

9 Jesus said to him, "Today salvation has come to this house, because this man, too, is a son of Abraham. 10 For the Son of Man came to seek and to save what was lost."

The Parable of the Ten Minas

11 While they were listening to this, he went on to tell them a parable, because he was near Jerusalem and the people thought that the kingdom of God was going to appear at once. 12 He said: "A man of noble birth went to a distant country to have himself appointed king and then to return. 13 So he called ten of his servants and gave them ten minas. 'Put this money to work,' he said, 'until I come back.'

14 "But his subjects hated him and sent a delegation after him to say, 'We don't want this man to be our king.'

15 "He was made king, however, and returned home. Then he sent for the servants to whom he had given the money, in order to find out what they had gained with it.

16 "The first one came and said, 'Sir, your mina has earned ten more.'

17 "'Well done, my good servant!' his master replied. 'Because you have been trustworthy in a very small matter, take charge of ten cities.'

18 "The second came and said, 'Sir, your mina has earned five more.'

19 "His master answered, 'You take charge of five cities.'

20 "Then another servant came and said, 'Sir, here is your mina; I have kept it laid away in a piece of cloth. 21 I was afraid of you, because you are a hard man. You take out what you did not put in and reap what you did not sow.'

22 "His master replied, 'I will judge you by your own words, you wicked servant! You knew, did you, that I am a hard man, taking out what I did not put in, and reaping what I did not sow? 23 Why then didn't you put my money on deposit, so that when I came back, I could have collected it with interest?'

24 "Then he said to those standing by, 'Take his mina away from him and give it to the one who has ten minas.'

25 "'Sir,' they said, 'he already has ten!'

26 "He replied, 'I tell you that to everyone who has, more will be given, but as for the one who has nothing, even what he has will be taken away. 27 But those enemies of mine who did not want me to be king over them—bring them here and kill them in front of me.'"

The Triumphal Entry

28 After Jesus had said this, he went on ahead, going up to Jerusalem. 29 As he approached Bethphage and Bethany at the hill called the Mount of Olives, he sent two of his disciples, saying to them, 30 "Go to the village ahead of you, and as you enter it, you will find a colt tied there, which no one has ever ridden. Untie it and bring it here. 31 If anyone asks you, 'Why are you untying it?' tell him, 'The Lord needs it.'"

32 Those who were sent ahead went and found it just as he had told them. 33 As they were untying the colt, its owners asked them, "Why are you untying the colt?"

34 They replied, "The Lord needs it."

35 They brought it to Jesus, threw their cloaks on the colt and put Jesus on it. 36 As he went along, people spread their cloaks on the road.

37 When he came near the place where the road goes down the Mount of Olives, the whole crowd of disciples began joyfully to praise God in loud voices for all the miracles they had seen: 38 "Blessed is the king who comes in the name of the Lord!" "Peace in heaven and glory in the highest!"

39 Some of the Pharisees in the crowd said to Jesus, "Teacher, rebuke your disciples!"

40 "I tell you," he replied, "if they keep quiet, the stones will cry out."

41 As he approached Jerusalem and saw the city, he wept over it 42 and said, "If you, even you, had only known on this day what would bring you peace—but now it is hidden from your eyes. 43 The days will come upon you when your enemies will build an embankment against you and encircle you and hem you in on every side. 44 They will dash you to the ground, you and the children within your walls. They will not leave one stone on another, because you did not recognize the time of God's coming to you."

Jesus at the Temple

45 Then he entered the temple area and began driving out those who were selling. 46 "It is written," he said to them, "'My house will be a house of prayer'; but you have made it 'a den of robbers.'"

47 Every day he was teaching at the temple. But the chief priests, the teachers of the law and the leaders among the people were trying to kill him. 48 Yet they could not find any way to do it, because all the people hung on his words.

DAY 26: JESUS IN DANGER—LUKE 20:1-47

CHAPTER 20

The Authority of Jesus Questioned

1 One day as he was teaching the people in the temple courts and preaching the Gospel, the chief priests and the teachers of the law, together with the elders, came up to him. 2 "Tell us by what authority you are doing these things," they said. "Who gave you this authority?"

3 He replied, "I will also ask you a question. Tell me, 4 John's baptism—was it from heaven, or from men?"

5 They discussed it among themselves and said, "If we say, 'From heaven,' he will ask, 'Why didn't you believe him?' 6 But if we say, 'From men,' all the people will stone us, because they are persuaded that John was a prophet."

7 So they answered, "We don't know where it was from."

8 Jesus said, "Neither will I tell you by what authority I am doing these things."

The Parable of the Tenants

9 He went on to tell the people this parable: "A man planted a vineyard, rented it to some farmers and went away for a long time. 10At harvest time he sent a servant to the tenants so they would give him some of the fruit of the vineyard. But the tenants beat him and sent him away empty-handed. 11 He sent another servant, but that one also they beat and treated shamefully and sent away empty-handed. 12 He sent still a third, and they wounded him and threw him out.

13 "Then the owner of the vineyard said, 'What shall I do? I will send my son, whom I love; perhaps they will respect him.'

14 "But when the tenants saw him, they talked the matter over. 'This is the heir,' they said. 'Let's kill him, and the inheritance will be ours.' 15 So they threw him out of the vineyard and killed him.

"What then will the owner of the vineyard do to them? 16 He will come and kill those tenants and give the vineyard to others." When the people heard this, they said, "May this never be!"

17 Jesus looked directly at them and asked, "Then what is the meaning of that which is written: 'The stone the builders rejected has become the capstone'? 18 Everyone who falls on that stone will be broken to pieces, but he on whom it falls will be crushed."

19 The teachers of the law and the chief priests looked for a way to arrest him immediately, because they knew he had spoken this parable against them. But they were afraid of the people.

▼

Paying Taxes to Caesar

20 Keeping a close watch on him, they sent spies, who pretended to be honest. They hoped to catch Jesus in something he said so that they might hand him over to the power and authority of the governor. 21 So the spies questioned him: "Teacher, we know that you speak and teach what is right, and that you do not show partiality but teach the way of God in accordance with the truth. 22 Is it right for us to pay taxes to Caesar or not?"

23 He saw through their duplicity and said to them, 24 "Show me a denarius. Whose portrait and inscription are on it?"

25 "Caesar's," they replied.

He said to them, "Then give to Caesar what is Caesar's, and to God what is God's."

26 They were unable to trap him in what he had said there in public. And astonished by his answer, they became silent.

The Resurrection and Marriage

27 Some of the Sadducees, who say there is no resurrection, came to Jesus with a question. 28 "Teacher," they said, "Moses wrote for us that if a man's brother dies and leaves a wife but no children, the man must marry the widow and have children for his brother. 29 Now there were seven brothers. The first one married a woman and died childless. 30 The second 31 and then the third married her, and in the same way the seven died, leaving no children. 32 Finally, the woman died too. 33 Now then, at the resurrection whose wife will she be, since the seven were married to her?"

34 Jesus replied, "The people of this age marry and are given in marriage. 35 But those who are considered worthy of taking part in that age and in the resurrection from the dead will neither marry nor be given in marriage, 36 and they can no longer die; for they are like the angels. They are God's children, since they are children of the resurrection. 37 But in the account of the bush, even Moses showed that

the dead rise, for he calls the Lord 'the God of Abraham, and the God of Isaac, and the God of Jacob.' 38 He is not the God of the dead, but of the living, for to him all are alive."

39 Some of the teachers of the law responded, "Well said, teacher!" 40 And no one dared to ask him any more questions.

Whose Son Is the Christ?

41 Then Jesus said to them, "How is it that they say the Christ is the Son of David? 42 David himself declares in the Book of Psalms: 'The Lord said to my Lord: "Sit at my right hand 43 until I make your enemies a footstool for your feet."' 44 David calls him 'Lord.' How then can he be his son?"

45 While all the people were listening, Jesus said to his disciples, 46 "Beware of the teachers of the law. They like to walk around in flowing robes and love to be greeted in the marketplaces and have the most important seats in the synagogues and the places of honor at banquets. 47 They devour widows' houses and for a show make lengthy prayers. Such men will be punished most severely."

DAY 27: "BE ALWAYS ON THE WATCH"—LUKE 21:1-38

CHAPTER 21

The Widow's Offering

1 As he looked up, Jesus saw the rich putting their gifts into the temple treasury. 2 He also saw a poor widow put in two very small copper coins. 3 "I tell you the truth," he said, "this poor widow has put in more than all the others. 4 All these people gave their gifts out of their wealth; but she out of her poverty put in all she had to live on."

Signs of the End of the Age

5 Some of his disciples were remarking about how the temple was adorned with beautiful stones and with gifts dedicated to God. But

Jesus said, 6 "As for what you see here, the time will come when not one stone will be left on another; every one of them will be thrown down."

7 "Teacher," they asked, "when will these things happen? And what will be the sign that they are about to take place?"

8 He replied: "Watch out that you are not deceived. For many will come in my name, claiming, 'I am he,' and, 'The time is near.' Do not follow them. 9 When you hear of wars and revolutions, do not be frightened. These things must happen first, but the end will not come right away."

10 Then he said to them: "Nation will rise against nation, and kingdom against kingdom. 11 There will be great earthquakes, famines and pestilences in various places, and fearful events and great signs from heaven.

12 "But before all this, they will lay hands on you and persecute you. They will deliver you to synagogues and prisons, and you will be brought before kings and governors, and all on account of my name. 13 This will result in your being witnesses to them. 14 But make up your mind not to worry beforehand how you will defend yourselves. 15 For I will give you words and wisdom that none of your adversaries will be able to resist or contradict. 16 You will be betrayed even by parents, brothers, relatives and friends, and they will put some of you to death. 17 All men will hate you because of me. 18 But not a hair of your head will perish. 19 By standing firm you will save yourselves.

20 "When you see Jerusalem surrounded by armies, you will know that its desolation is near. 21 Then let those who are in Judea flee to the mountains, let those in the city get out, and let those in the country not enter the city. 22 For this is the time of punishment in fulfillment of all that has been written. 23 How dreadful it will be in those days for pregnant women and nursing mothers! There will be great distress in the land and wrath against this people. 24 They will fall by the sword and will be taken as prisoners to all the nations. Jerusalem will be trampled on by the Gentiles until the times of the Gentiles are fulfilled.

25 "There will be signs in the sun, moon and stars. On the earth, nations will be in anguish and perplexity at the roaring and tossing of the sea. 26 Men will faint from terror, apprehensive of what is coming on the world, for the heavenly bodies will be shaken. 27 At that time they will see the Son of Man coming in a cloud with power and great glory. 28 When these things begin to take place, stand up and lift up your heads, because your redemption is drawing near."

29 He told them this parable: "Look at the fig tree and all the trees. 30 When they sprout leaves, you can see for yourselves and know that summer is near. 31 Even so, when you see these things happening, you know that the kingdom of God is near.

32 "I tell you the truth, this generation will certainly not pass away until all these things have happened. 33 Heaven and earth will pass away, but my words will never pass away.

34 "Be careful, or your hearts will be weighed down with dissipation, drunkenness and the anxieties of life, and that day will close on you unexpectedly like a trap. 35 For it will come upon all those who live on the face of the whole earth. 36 Be always on the watch, and pray that you may be able to escape all that is about to happen, and that you may be able to stand before the Son of Man."

37 Each day Jesus was teaching at the temple, and each evening he went out to spend the night on the hill called the Mount of Olives, 38and all the people came early in the morning to hear him at the temple.

DAY 28: JESUS ON TRIAL—LUKE 22:1-71

CHAPTER 22

Judas Agrees to Betray Jesus

1 Now the Feast of Unleavened Bread, called the Passover, was approaching, 2 and the chief priests and the teachers of the law were looking for some way to get rid of Jesus, for they were afraid of the

people. ³ Then Satan entered Judas, called Iscariot, one of the Twelve. ⁴ And Judas went to the chief priests and the officers of the temple guard and discussed with them how he might betray Jesus. ⁵ They were delighted and agreed to give him money. ⁶ He consented, and watched for an opportunity to hand Jesus over to them when no crowd was present.

The Last Supper

⁷ Then came the day of Unleavened Bread on which the Passover lamb had to be sacrificed. ⁸ Jesus sent Peter and John, saying, "Go and make preparations for us to eat the Passover."

⁹ "Where do you want us to prepare for it?" they asked.

¹⁰ He replied, "As you enter the city, a man carrying a jar of water will meet you. Follow him to the house that he enters, ¹¹ and say to the owner of the house, 'The Teacher asks: Where is the guest room, where I may eat the Passover with my disciples?' ¹² He will show you a large upper room, all furnished. Make preparations there."

¹³ They left and found things just as Jesus had told them. So they prepared the Passover.

¹⁴ When the hour came, Jesus and his apostles reclined at the table. ¹⁵ And he said to them, "I have eagerly desired to eat this Passover with you before I suffer. ¹⁶ For I tell you, I will not eat it again until it finds fulfillment in the kingdom of God."

¹⁷ After taking the cup, he gave thanks and said, "Take this and divide it among you. ¹⁸ For I tell you I will not drink again of the fruit of the vine until the kingdom of God comes."

¹⁹ And he took bread, gave thanks and broke it, and gave it to them, saying, "This is my body given for you; do this in remembrance of me."

²⁰ In the same way, after the supper he took the cup, saying, "This cup is the new covenant in my blood, which is poured out for you. ²¹But the hand of him who is going to betray me is with mine on the

table. 22 The Son of Man will go as it has been decreed, but woe to that man who betrays him." 23 They began to question among themselves which of them it might be who would do this.

24 Also a dispute arose among them as to which of them was considered to be greatest. 25 Jesus said to them, "The kings of the Gentiles lord it over them; and those who exercise authority over them call themselves Benefactors. 26 But you are not to be like that. Instead, the greatest among you should be like the youngest, and the one who rules like the one who serves. 27 For who is greater, the one who is at the table or the one who serves? Is it not the one who is at the table? But I am among you as one who serves. 28 You are those who have stood by me in my trials. 29 And I confer on you a kingdom, just as my Father conferred one on me, 30 so that you may eat and drink at my table in my kingdom and sit on thrones, judging the twelve tribes of Israel.

31 "Simon, Simon, Satan has asked to sift you as wheat. 32 But I have prayed for you, Simon, that your faith may not fail. And when you have turned back, strengthen your brothers."

33 But he replied, "Lord, I am ready to go with you to prison and to death."

34 Jesus answered, "I tell you, Peter, before the rooster crows today, you will deny three times that you know me."

35 Then Jesus asked them, "When I sent you without purse, bag or sandals, did you lack anything?"

"Nothing," they answered.

36 He said to them, "But now if you have a purse, take it, and also a bag; and if you don't have a sword, sell your cloak and buy one. 37 It is written: 'And he was numbered with the transgressors'; and I tell you that this must be fulfilled in me. Yes, what is written about me is reaching its fulfillment."

38 The disciples said, "See, Lord, here are two swords."

"That is enough," he replied.

Jesus Prays on the Mount of Olives

39 Jesus went out as usual to the Mount of Olives, and his disciples followed him. 40 On reaching the place, he said to them, "Pray that you will not fall into temptation." 41 He withdrew about a stone's throw beyond them, knelt down and prayed, 42 "Father, if you are willing, take this cup from me; yet not my will, but yours be done." 43 An angel from heaven appeared to him and strengthened him. 44 And being in anguish, he prayed more earnestly, and his sweat was like drops of blood falling to the ground.

45 When he rose from prayer and went back to the disciples, he found them asleep, exhausted from sorrow. 46 "Why are you sleeping?" he asked them. "Get up and pray so that you will not fall into temptation."

Jesus Arrested

47 While he was still speaking a crowd came up, and the man who was called Judas, one of the Twelve, was leading them. He approached Jesus to kiss him, 48 but Jesus asked him, "Judas, are you betraying the Son of Man with a kiss?"

49 When Jesus' followers saw what was going to happen, they said, "Lord, should we strike with our swords?" 50 And one of them struck the servant of the high priest, cutting off his right ear.

51 But Jesus answered, "No more of this!" And he touched the man's ear and healed him.

52 Then Jesus said to the chief priests, the officers of the temple guard, and the elders, who had come for him, "Am I leading a rebellion, that you have come with swords and clubs? 53 Every day I was with you in the temple courts, and you did not lay a hand on me. But this is your hour—when darkness reigns."

Peter Disowns Jesus

54 Then seizing him, they led him away and took him into the house of the high priest. Peter followed at a distance. 55 But when they

had kindled a fire in the middle of the courtyard and had sat down together, Peter sat down with them. 56 A servant girl saw him seated there in the firelight. She looked closely at him and said, "This man was with him."

57 But he denied it. "Woman, I don't know him," he said.

58 A little later someone else saw him and said, "You also are one of them."

"Man, I am not!" Peter replied.

59 About an hour later another asserted, "Certainly this fellow was with him, for he is a Galilean."

60 Peter replied, "Man, I don't know what you're talking about!" Just as he was speaking, the rooster crowed. 61 The Lord turned and looked straight at Peter. Then Peter remembered the word the Lord had spoken to him: "Before the rooster crows today, you will disown me three times." 62 And he went outside and wept bitterly.

The Soldiers Mock Jesus

63 The men who were guarding Jesus began mocking and beating him. 64 They blindfolded him and demanded, "Prophesy! Who hit you?" 65 And they said many other insulting things to him.

Jesus Before the Council of the Jews

66 At daybreak the council of the elders of the people, both the chief priests and teachers of the law, met together, and Jesus was led before them. 67 "If you are the Christ," they said, "tell us."

Jesus answered, "If I tell you, you will not believe me, 68 and if I asked you, you would not answer. 69 But from now on, the Son of Man will be seated at the right hand of the mighty God."

70 They all asked, "Are you then the Son of God?"

He replied, "You are right in saying I am."

71 Then they said, "Why do we need any more testimony? We have heard it from his own lips."

DAY 29: JESUS IS CRUCIFIED—LUKE 23:1-56

CHAPTER 23

Jesus Before Pilate and Herod

1 Then the whole assembly rose and led him off to Pilate. 2 And they began to accuse him, saying, "We have found this man subverting our nation. He opposes payment of taxes to Caesar and claims to be Christ, a king."

3 So Pilate asked Jesus, "Are you the king of the Jews?"

"Yes, it is as you say," Jesus replied.

4 Then Pilate announced to the chief priests and the crowd, "I find no basis for a charge against this man."

5 But they insisted, "He stirs up the people all over Judea by his teaching. He started in Galilee and has come all the way here."

6 On hearing this, Pilate asked if the man was a Galilean. 7 When he learned that Jesus was under Herod's jurisdiction, he sent him to Herod, who was also in Jerusalem at that time.

8 When Herod saw Jesus, he was greatly pleased, because for a long time he had been wanting to see him. From what he had heard about him, he hoped to see him perform some miracle. 9 He plied him with many questions, but Jesus gave him no answer. 10 The chief priests and the teachers of the law were standing there, vehemently accusing him. 11 Then Herod and his soldiers ridiculed and mocked him. Dressing him in an elegant robe, they sent him back to Pilate. 12 That day Herod and Pilate became friends—before this they had been enemies.

13 Pilate called together the chief priests, the rulers and the people, 14 and said to them, "You brought me this man as one who was inciting the people to rebellion. I have examined him in your presence and have found no basis for your charges against him. 15 Neither has Herod, for he sent him back to us; as you can see, he has done nothing to deserve death. 16 Therefore, I will punish him and then release him."

18 With one voice they cried out, "Away with this man! Release Barabbas to us!" 19 (Barabbas had been thrown into prison for an insurrection in the city, and for murder.)

20 Wanting to release Jesus, Pilate appealed to them again. 21 But they kept shouting, "Crucify him! Crucify him!"

22 For the third time he spoke to them: "Why? What crime has this man committed? I have found in him no grounds for the death penalty. Therefore I will have him punished and then release him."

23 But with loud shouts they insistently demanded that he be crucified, and their shouts prevailed. 24 So Pilate decided to grant their demand. 25 He released the man who had been thrown into prison for insurrection and murder, the one they asked for, and surrendered Jesus to their will.

The Crucifixion

26 As they led him away, they seized Simon from Cyrene, who was on his way in from the country, and put the cross on him and made him carry it behind Jesus. 27 A large number of people followed him, including women who mourned and wailed for him. 28 Jesus turned and said to them, "Daughters of Jerusalem, do not weep for me; weep for yourselves and for your children. 29 For the time will come when you will say, 'Blessed are the barren women, the wombs that never bore and the breasts that never nursed!' 30 Then 'they will say to the mountains, "Fall on us!" and to the hills, "Cover us!"' 31 For if men do these things when the tree is green, what will happen when it is dry?"

32 Two other men, both criminals, were also led out with him to be executed. 33 When they came to the place called The Skull, there they crucified him, along with the criminals—one on his right, the other on his left. 34 Jesus said, "Father, forgive them, for they do not know what they are doing." And they divided up his clothes by casting lots.

35 The people stood watching, and the rulers even sneered at him.

They said, "He saved others; let him save himself if he is the Christ of God, the Chosen One."

36 The soldiers also came up and mocked him. They offered him wine vinegar 37 and said, "If you are the king of the Jews, save yourself."

38 There was a written notice above him, which read: THIS IS THE KING OF THE JEWS.

39 One of the criminals who hung there hurled insults at him: "Aren't you the Christ? Save yourself and us!"

40 But the other criminal rebuked him. "Don't you fear God," he said, "since you are under the same sentence? 41 We are punished justly, for we are getting what our deeds deserve. But this man has done nothing wrong."

42 Then he said, "Jesus, remember me when you come into your kingdom."

43 Jesus answered him, "I tell you the truth, today you will be with me in paradise."

Jesus' Death

44 It was now about the sixth hour, and darkness came over the whole land until the ninth hour, 45 for the sun stopped shining. And the curtain of the temple was torn in two. 46 Jesus called out with a loud voice, "Father, into your hands I commit my spirit." When he had said this, he breathed his last.

47 The centurion, seeing what had happened, praised God and said, "Surely this was a righteous man." 48 When all the people who had gathered to witness this sight saw what took place, they beat their breasts and went away. 49 But all those who knew him, including the women who had followed him from Galilee, stood at a distance, watching these things.

Jesus' Burial

50 Now there was a man named Joseph, a member of the Council, a good and upright man, 51 who had not consented to their decision

▼

and action. He came from the Judean town of Arimathea and he was waiting for the kingdom of God. [52] Going to Pilate, he asked for Jesus' body. [53] Then he took it down, wrapped it in linen cloth and placed it in a tomb cut in the rock, one in which no one had yet been laid. [54] It was Preparation Day, and the Sabbath was about to begin.

[55] The women who had come with Jesus from Galilee followed Joseph and saw the tomb and how his body was laid in it. [56] Then they went home and prepared spices and perfumes. But they rested on the Sabbath in obedience to the commandment.

DAY 30: JESUS IS ALIVE!—LUKE 24:1-53

CHAPTER 24

The Resurrection

[1] On the first day of the week, very early in the morning, the women took the spices they had prepared and went to the tomb. [2] They found the stone rolled away from the tomb, [3] but when they entered, they did not find the body of the Lord Jesus. [4] While they were wondering about this, suddenly two men in clothes that gleamed like lightning stood beside them. [5] In their fright the women bowed down with their faces to the ground, but the men said to them, "Why do you look for the living among the dead? [6] He is not here; he has risen! Remember how he told you, while he was still with you in Galilee: [7] 'The Son of Man must be delivered into the hands of sinful men, be crucified and on the third day be raised again.'" [8] Then they remembered his words.

[9] When they came back from the tomb, they told all these things to the Eleven and to all the others. [10] It was Mary Magdalene, Joanna, Mary the mother of James, and the others with them who told this to the apostles. [11] But they did not believe the women, because their words seemed to them like nonsense. [12] Peter, however, got up and ran to the tomb. Bending over, he saw the strips of

▼

linen lying by themselves, and he went away, wondering to himself what had happened.

On the Road to Emmaus

13 Now that same day two of them were going to a village called Emmaus, about seven miles from Jerusalem. 14 They were talking with each other about everything that had happened. 15 As they talked and discussed these things with each other, Jesus himself came up and walked along with them; 16 but they were kept from recognizing him.

17 He asked them, "What are you discussing together as you walk along?"

They stood still, their faces downcast. 18 One of them, named Cleopas, asked him, "Are you the only one living in Jerusalem who doesn't know the things that have happened there in these days?"

19 "What things?" he asked.

"About Jesus of Nazareth," they replied. "He was a prophet, powerful in word and deed before God and all the people. 20 The chief priests and our rulers handed him over to be sentenced to death, and they crucified him; 21 but we had hoped that he was the one who was going to redeem Israel. And what is more, it is the third day since all this took place. 22 In addition, some of our women amazed us. They went to the tomb early this morning 23 but didn't find his body. They came and told us that they had seen a vision of angels, who said he was alive. 24 Then some of our companions went to the tomb and found it just as the women had said, but him they did not see."

25 He said to them, "How foolish you are, and how slow of heart to believe all that the prophets have spoken! 26 Did not the Christ have to suffer these things and then enter his glory?" 27 And beginning with Moses and all the Prophets, he explained to them what was said in all the Scriptures concerning himself.

28 As they approached the village to which they were going, Jesus acted as if he were going farther. 29 But they urged him strongly, "Stay

with us, for it is nearly evening; the day is almost over." So he went in to stay with them.

30 When he was at the table with them, he took bread, gave thanks, broke it and began to give it to them. 31 Then their eyes were opened and they recognized him, and he disappeared from their sight. 32 They asked each other, "Were not our hearts burning within us while he talked with us on the road and opened the Scriptures to us?"

33 They got up and returned at once to Jerusalem. There they found the Eleven and those with them, assembled together 34 and saying, "It is true! The Lord has risen and has appeared to Simon." 35Then the two told what had happened on the way, and how Jesus was recognized by them when he broke the bread.

Jesus Appears to the Disciples

36 While they were still talking about this, Jesus himself stood among them and said to them, "Peace be with you."

37 They were startled and frightened, thinking they saw a ghost. 38 He said to them, "Why are you troubled, and why do doubts rise in your minds? 39 Look at my hands and my feet. It is I myself! Touch me and see; a ghost does not have flesh and bones, as you see I have."

40 When he had said this, he showed them his hands and feet. 41And while they still did not believe it because of joy and amazement, he asked them, "Do you have anything here to eat?" 42 They gave him a piece of broiled fish, 43 and he took it and ate it in their presence.

44 He said to them, "This is what I told you while I was still with you: Everything must be fulfilled that is written about me in the Law of Moses, the Prophets and the Psalms."

45 Then he opened their minds so they could understand the Scriptures. 46 He told them, "This is what is written: The Christ will suffer and rise from the dead on the third day, 47 and repentance and forgiveness of sins will be preached in his name to all nations, begin-

ning at Jerusalem. [48] You are witnesses of these things. [49] I am going
to send you what my Father has promised; but stay in the city until
you have been clothed with power from on high."

The Ascension

[50] When he had led them out to the vicinity of Bethany, he lifted
up his hands and blessed them. [51] While he was blessing them, he left
them and was taken up into heaven. [52] Then they worshiped him and
returned to Jerusalem with great joy. [53] And they stayed continually
at the temple, praising God.

Resources

Your Daily Bible Study: A 365-day Reading Plan for Enjoying Your Bible

This is an easy-to-follow Bible reading plan developed by Robert Murray M'Cheyne, a nineteenth-century Scottish minister known for his holiness, humility, and unfaltering devotional life. His love for the Bible and devotion to God has marked my life and ministry.

Born in 1813 in Edinburgh, Scotland, M'Cheyne died at the age of twenty-nine. Yet in his short lifetime, because of his holiness, humility, and anxious efforts to save souls, he made a lasting impression on society.

The need for personal holiness before God so impressed M'Cheyne that he wrote, "According to your holiness, so shall be your success. . . . A holy man is an awesome weapon in the hand of God."

Many factors make a lasting impact for good on a community or nation. But holiness among the people of God, particularly among the leadership, is fundamental. Sin—a lack of holiness—grieves the Holy Spirit and hinders His work. Scripture warns, "Do not grieve the Holy Spirit" (Ephesians 4:30) and "Do not put out the Spirit's fire" (1 Thessalonians 5:19).

On the other hand, Scripture exhorts us, "Be filled with the Spirit"

(Ephesians 5:18). To be filled with the Spirit is a command, a duty, and a privilege for the Christian. To be filled with the Spirit means to be walking in His light and to be controlled by the indwelling Lord. To do this we must spend time every day reading and studying the Bible, filling our minds and hearts with the life-changing, inspired Word of God (see Colossians 3:16).

To encourage holy, Spirit-filled living among his congregation, M'Cheyne developed and published this daily reading guide. He urged fellow believers to read Holy Scripture "in all its breadth!"

How about you? Have you disciplined yourself to read the Bible each day? If not, start today!

J A N U A R Y				
Morning		Day	Evening	
Gen. 1	Matt. 1	1	Ezra 1	Acts 1
2	2	2	2	2
3	3	3	3	3
4	4	4	4	4
5	5	5	5	5
6	6	6	6	6
7	7	7	7	7
8	8	8	8	8
9-10	9	9	9	9
11	10	10	10	10
12	11	11	Neh. 1	11
13	12	12	2	12
14	13	13	3	13
15	14	14	4	14
16	15	15	5	15
17	16	16	6	16
18	17	17	7	17
19	18	18	8	18
20	19	19	9	19
21	20	20	10	20
22	21	21	11	21
23	22	22	12	22
24	23	23	13	23
25	24	24	Esther 1	24
26	25	25	2	25
27	26	26	3	26
28	27	27	4	27
29	28	28	5	28
30	Mark 1	29	6	Rom. 1
31	2	30	7	2
32	3	31	8	3

This is my beloved son, with whom I am
well pleased; listen to him.

F E B R U A R Y				
Morning		Day	Evening	
Gen. 33	Mark 4	1	Esther 9-10	Rom. 4
34	5	2	Job 1	5
35-36	6	3	2	6
37	7	4	3	7
38	8	5	4	8
39	9	6	5	9
40	10	7	6	10
41	11	8	7	11
42	12	9	8	12
43	13	10	9	13
44	14	11	10	14
45	15	12	11	15
46	16	13	12	16
47	Luke 1:1-38	14	13	1 Cor. 1
48	1:39-80	15	14	2
49	2	16	15	3
50	3	17	16-17	4
Ex. 1	4	18	18	5
2	5	19	19	6
3	6	20	20	7
4	7	21	21	8
5	8	22	22	9
6	9	23	23	10
7	10	24	24	11
8	11	25	25-26	12
9	12	26	27	13
10	13	27	28	14
11-12:20	14	28	29	15

I have esteemed the words of his mouth
more than my necessary food.

M A R C H				
Morning		Day	Evening	
Ex.12:21-51	Luke 15	1	Job 30	1 Cor. 16
13	16	2	31	2 Cor. 1
14	17	3	32	2
15	18	4	33	3
16	19	5	34	4
17	20	6	35	5
18	21	7	36	6
19	22	8	37	7
20	23	9	38	8
21	24	10	39	9
22	John 1	11	40	10
23	2	12	41	11
24	3	13	42	12
25	4	14	Prov. 1	13
26	5	15	2	Gal. 1
27	6	16	3	2
28	7	17	4	3
29	8	18	5	4
30	9	19	6	5
31	10	20	7	6
32	11	21	8	Eph. 1
33	12	22	9	2
34	13	23	10	3
35	14	24	11	4
36	15	25	12	5
37	16	26	13	6
38	17	27	14	Phil. 1
39	18	28	15	2
40	19	29	16	3
Lev. 1	20	30	17	4
2-3	21	31	18	Col. 1

Mary kept all these things, pondering them in her heart.

A P R I L				
Morning		Day	Evening	
Lev. 4	Ps. 1-2	1	Prov. 19	Col. 2
5	3-4	2	20	3
6	5-6	3	21	4
7	7-8	4	22	1 Thess. 1
8	9	5	23	2
9	10	6	24	3
10	11-12	7	25	4
11-12	13-14	8	26	5
13	15-16	9	27	2 Thess. 1
14	17	10	28	2
15	18	11	29	3
16	19	12	30	1 Tim. 1
17	20-21	13	31	2
18	22	14	Eccles. 1	3
19	23-24	15	2	4
20	25	16	3	5
21	26-27	17	4	6
22	28-29	18	5	2 Tim. 1
23	30	19	6	2
24	31	20	7	3
25	32	21	8	4
26	33	22	9	Titus 1
27	34	23	10	2
Num. 1	35	24	11	3
2	36	25	12	Philem.
3	37	26	Song 1	Heb. 1
4	38	27	2	2
5	39	28	3	3
6	40-41	29	4	4
7	42-43	30	5	5

O send out thy light and thy truth; let them lead me.

M	A	Y		
Morning		Day	Evening	
Num. 8	Ps. 44	1	Song 6	Heb. 6
9	45	2	7	7
10	46-47	3	8	8
11	48	4	Isa. 1	9
12-13	49	5	2	10
14	50	6	3-4	11
15	51	7	5	12
16	52-54	8	6	13
17-18	55	9	7	James 1
19	56-57	10	8-9:7	2
20	58-59	11	9:8-10:4	3
21	60-61	12	10:5-34	4
22	62-63	13	11-12	5
23	64-65	14	13	1 Pet. 1
24	66-67	15	14	2
25	68	16	15	3
26	69	17	16	4
27	70-71	18	17-18	5
28	72	19	19-20	2 Pet. 1
29	73	20	21	2
30	74	21	22	3
31	75-76	22	23	1 John 1
32	77	23	24	2
33	78:1-37	24	25	3
34	78:38-72	25	26	4
35	79	26	27	5
36	80	27	28	2 John
Deut. 1	81-82	28	29	3 John
2	83-84	29	30	Jude
3	85	30	31	Rev. 1
4	86-87	31	32	2

From a child thou hast known the holy scriptures.

J U N E				
Morning		Day	Evening	
Deut. 5	Ps. 88	1	Isa. 33	Rev. 3
6	89	2	34	4
7	90	3	35	5
8	91	4	36	6
9	92-93	5	37	7
10	94	6	38	8
11	95-96	7	39	9
12	97-98	8	40	10
13-14	99-101	9	41	11
15	102	10	42	12
16	103	11	43	13
17	104	12	44	14
18	105	13	45	15
19	106	14	46	16
20	107	15	47	17
21	108-109	16	48	18
22	110-111	17	49	19
23	112-113	18	50	20
24	114-115	19	51	21
25	116	20	52	22
26	117-118	21	53	Matt. 1
27-28:19	119:1-24	22	54	2
28:20-68	119:25-48	23	55	3
29	119:49-72	24	56	4
30	119:73-96	25	57	5
31	119:97-120	26	58	6
32	119:121-144	27	59	7
33-34	119:145-176	28	60	8
Josh. 1	120-122	29	61	9
2	123-125	30	62	10

Blessed is he that readeth and they that hear.

J U L Y				
Morning		Day	Evening	
Josh. 3	Ps. 126-128	1	Isa. 63	Matt. 11
4	129-131	2	64	12
5-6:5	132-134	3	65	13
6:6-27	135-136	4	66	14
7	137-138	5	Jer. 1	15
8	139	6	2	16
9	140-141	7	3	17
10	142-143	8	4	18
11	144	9	5	19
12-13	145	10	6	20
14-15	146-147	11	7	21
16-17	148	12	8	22
18-19	149-150	13	9	23
20-21	Acts 1	14	10	24
22	2	15	11	25
23	3	16	12	26
24	4	17	13	27
Judg. 1	5	18	14	28
2	6	19	15	Mark 1
3	7	20	16	2
4	8	21	17	3
5	9	22	18	4
6	10	23	19	5
7	11	24	20	6
8	12	25	21	7
9	13	26	22	8
10-11:11	14	27	23	9
11:12-40	15	28	24	10
12	16	29	25	11
13	17	30	26	12
14	18	31	27	13

They received the word with all readiness of mind,
and searched the scriptures daily.

A U G U S T				
Morning		Day	Evening	
Judg. 15	Acts 19	1	Jer. 28	Mark 14
16	20	2	29	15
17	21	3	30-31	16
18	22	4	32	Ps. 1-2
19	23	5	33	3-4
20	24	6	34	5-6
21	25	7	35	7-8
Ruth 1	26	8	36	9
2	27	9	37	10
3-4	28	10	38	11-12
1 Sam. 1	Rom. 1	11	39	13-14
2	2	12	40	15-16
3	3	13	41	17
4	4	14	42	18
5-6	5	15	43	19
7-8	6	16	44	20-21
9	7	17	45	22
10	8	18	46	23-24
11	9	19	47	25
12	10	20	48	26-27
13	11	21	49	28-29
14	12	22	50	30
15	13	23	51	31
16	14	24	52	32
17	15	25	Lam. 1	33
18	16	26	2	34
19	1 Cor. 1	27	3	35
20	2	28	4	36
21-22	3	29	5	37
23	4	30	Ezek. 1	38
24	5	31	2-3	39

Speak, Lord; for thy servant heareth.

S E P T E M B E R				
Morning		Day	Evening	
1 Sam. 25	1 Cor. 6	1	Ezek. 4	Ps. 40-41
26	7	2	5	42-43
27	8	3	6	44
28	9	4	7	45
29-30	10	5	8	46-47
31	11	6	9	48
2 Sam. 1	12	7	10	49
2	13	8	11	50
3	14	9	12	51
4-5	15	10	13	52-54
6	16	11	14	55
7	2 Cor. 1	12	15	56-57
8-9	2	13	16	58-59
10	3	14	17	60-61
11	4	15	18	62-63
12	5	16	19	64-65
13	6	17	20	66-67
14	7	18	21	68
15	8	19	22	69
16	9	20	23	70-71
17	10	21	24	72
18	11	22	25	73
19	12	23	26	74
20	13	24	27	75-76
21	Gal. 1	25	28	77
22	2	26	29	78:1-37
23	3	27	30	78:38-72
24	4	28	31	79
1 Kgs. 1	5	29	32	80
2	6	30	33	81-82

The law of the Lord is perfect, converting the soul.

Morning		Day	Evening	
O	C	T O B E R		
1 Kgs. 3	Eph.1	1	Ezek. 34	Ps. 83-84
4-5	2	2	35	85
6	3	3	36	86
7	4	4	37	87-88
8	5	5	38	89
9	6	6	39	90
10	Phil. 1	7	40	91
11	2	8	41	92-93
12	3	9	42	94
13	4	10	43	95-96
14	Col.1	11	44	97-98
15	2	12	45	99-101
16	3	13	46	102
17	4	14	47	103
18	1 Thess. 1	15	48	104
19	2	16	Dan. 1	105
20	3	17	2	106
21	4	18	3	107
22	5	19	4	108-109
2 Kgs. 1	2 Thess. 1	20	5	110-111
2	2	21	6	112-113
3	3	22	7	114-115
4	1 Tim. 1	23	8	116
5	2	24	9	117-118
6	3	25	10	119:1-24
7	4	26	11	119:25-48
8	5	27	12	119:49-72
9	6	28	Hos. 1	119:73-96
10	2 Tim. 1	29	2	119:97-120
11-12	2	30	3-4	119:121-144
13	3	31	5-6	119:145-176

O how I love thy law! It is my meditation all the day.

N O V E M B E R				
Morning		Day	Evening	
2 Kgs. 14	2 Tim. 4	1	Hos. 7	Ps. 120-122
15	Titus 1	2	8	123-125
16	2	3	9	126-128
17	3	4	10	129-131
18	Philem.	5	11	132-134
19	Heb. 1	6	12	135-136
20	2	7	13	137-138
21	3	8	14	139
22	4	9	Joel 1	140-141
23	5	10	2	142
24	6	11	3	143
25	7	12	Amos 1	144
1 Chron. 1-2	8	13	2	145
3-4	9	14	3	146-147
5-6	10	15	4	148-150
7-8	11	16	5	Lk. 1:1-38
9-10	12	17	6	1:39-80
11-12	13	18	7	2
13-14	James 1	19	8	3
15	2	20	9	4
16	3	21	Obad.	5
17	4	22	Jonah 1	6
18	5	23	2	7
19-20	1 Pet. 1	24	3	8
21	2	25	4	9
22	3	26	Micah 1	10
23	4	27	2	11
24-25	5	28	3	12
26-27	2 Pet. 1	29	4	13
28	2	30	5	14

As newborn babes, desire the sincere milk of the word
that ye may grow thereby.

D E C E M B E R		Day	Evening	
Morning				
1 Chron. 29	2 Peter 3	1	Micah 6	Luke 15
2 Chron. 1	1 John 1	2	7	16
2	2	3	Nahum 1	17
3-4	3	4	2	18
5-6:11	4	5	3	19
6:12-42	5	6	Hab. 1	20
7	2 John	7	2	21
8	3 John	8	3	22
9	Jude	9	Zeph. 1	23
10	Rev. 1	10	2	24
11-12	2	11	3	John 1
13	3	12	Hag. 1	2
14-15	4	13	2	3
16	5	14	Zech. 1	4
17	6	15	2	5
18	7	16	3	6
19-20	8	17	4	7
21	9	18	5	8
22-23	10	19	6	9
24	11	20	7	10
25	12	21	8	11
26	13	22	9	12
27-28	14	23	10	13
29	15	24	11	14
30	16	25	12-13:1	15
31	17	26	13:2-9	16
32	18	27	14	17
33	19	28	Mal. 1	18
34	20	29	2	19
35	21	30	3	20
36	22	31	4	21

The law of his God is in his heart; none of his steps shall slide.

Recommended Reading

To continue growing in your Christian faith, keep reading! I encourage you to look for these and other helpful books at your local Christian bookstore.

Almanac of the Christian World (Wheaton, Ill.: Tyndale House).
The Art of Sharing Your Faith by Joel D. Heck, editor (Grand Rapids, Mich.: Revell).
Breaking Down Walls by Raleigh Washington and Glen Hehrein (Chicago: Moody Press).
Calling America and the Nations to Christ by Luis Palau (Nashville: Thomas Nelson).
Finding Friendship with God by Floyd McClung (Ann Arbor, Mich.: Vine Books).
The Greatest Lesson I've Ever Learned (San Bernardino, Calif.: Here's Life).
Half Time by Bob Buford (Grand Rapids, Mich.: Zondervan).
Healthy Habits for Spiritual Growth by Luis Palau (Grand Rapids, Mich.: Discovery House).

Heaven Help the Home by Howard G. Hendricks (Wheaton, Ill.: Victor Books).

Husbands and Wives by Howard and Jeanne Hendricks, general editors (Wheaton, Ill.: Victor Books).

Jesus Works Here by Robert J. Tamasy, editor (Nashville: Broadman & Holman).

Keeping Your Kids Christian by Marshall Shelley (Ann Arbor, Mich.: Vine Books).

Measure Your Life by Wesley L. Duewel (Grand Rapids, Mich.: Zondervan).

More than Conquerors by John Woodbridge, general editor (Chicago: Moody Press).

The Only Hope for America by Luis Palau (Wheaton, Ill.: Crossway Books).

Operation World by Patrick Johnstone (Grand Rapids, Mich.: Zondervan).

Playing the Odds by Jay Carty (Ventura, Calif.: Vision House).

Practical Christianity. (Wheaton, Ill.: Tyndale House).

Racing Toward 2001 by Russell Chandler (Grand Rapids, Mich.: Zondervan).

Say Yes! How to Renew Your Spiritual Passion by Luis Palau (Grand Rapids, Mich.: Discovery House).

Seven Promises of a Promise Keeper (Colorado Springs: Focus on the Family).

Promises Promises (Gresham, Ore.: Vision House).

Surprise Endings by Ron Mehl (San Diego: Questar).

What Good Parents Have in Common by Janis Long Harris (Grand Rapids, Mich.: Zondervan).

What Makes a Man (Colorado Springs: NavPress).

By the way, when a relative or friend trusts Jesus Christ, be sure to give him or her a copy of this book.

Of course, the most important book to read each day is *The Holy Bible*, available in both traditional and contemporary translations.